Systemic and Narrative Work with Unaccompanied Asylum-Seeking Children

Systemic and Narrative Work with Unaccompanied Asylum-Seeking Children: Stories of Relocation provides a contextualised, research-based understanding of how to enhance and support the emotional health and well-being of unaccompanied asylum-seeking children.

The framework presented in this book is an innovative intervention that enhances the well-being of children who have experienced trauma by improving the therapeutic abilities for all who support and care for them. This book presents the evidence base for this new systemic and narrative trauma-informed framework of care, creates a wider understanding of working with trauma responses in unaccompanied asylum-seeking children and offers coherence for practitioners wanting to use this approach. The authors provide a physiological view, as well as identify embodied aspects of trauma experience, and describe a narrative approach developed from a clinical understanding of trauma, as well as presenting the words of children who took part in the project. Creating a common multi-disciplinary language, this approach can be used to improve coherence, coordination, and excellence within the whole system.

This book is essential reading for all practitioners working with unaccompanied asylum-seeking children. It will also be of interest to students and trainees of social work and other mental health disciplines, as well as other professionals seeking to understand the needs of this group.

Ana Draper, DSysPsych (Doctorate in Systemic Psychotherapy), is a consultant systemic psychotherapist and supervisor at the Tavistock and Portman NHS Foundation trust, UK, Founding Member of Improved Futures, and CMM fellow.

Elisa Marcellino is a clinical, counselling and health psychologist (HCPC) and CMM Fellow. Elisa works as senior clinician in a South East London National Health Trust.

Samantha Thomson is a systemic psychotherapist and family therapist in a South East London National Health Trust, and CMM fellow.

The Systemic Thinking and Practice Series

Series Editors: Charlotte Burck and Gwyn Daniel

This influential series was co-founded in 1989 by series editors David Campbell and Ros Draper to promote innovative applications of systemic theory to psychotherapy, teaching, supervision and organisational consultation. In 2011, Charlotte Burck and Gwyn Daniel became series editors and aim to present new theoretical developments and pioneering practice, to make links with other theoretical approaches, and to promote the relevance of systemic theory to contemporary social and psychological questions.

Recent titles in the series include:

Creative Positions in Adult Mental Health: Outside In-Inside Out
Edited by Sue McNab and Karen Partridge

Ethical and Aesthetic Explorations of Systemic Practice: New Critical Reflections
Pietro Barbetta, Maria Esther Cavagnis, Inga-Britt Krause and Umberta Telfener

Working Systemically with Refugee Couples and Families: Exploring Trauma, Resilience and Culture
Shadi Shahnavaz

Psychotherapeutic Competencies: Techniques, Relationships, and Epistemology in Systemic Practice
Laura Fruggeri, Francesca Balestra, and Elena Venturelli

Systemic Perspectives in Mental Health, Social Work and Youth Care
Anke Savenije, Justine van Lawick, and Ellen Reijmers

Systemic and Narrative Work with Unaccompanied Asylum-Seeking Children: Stories of Relocation
Ana Draper, Elisa Marcellino, and Samantha Thomson

Systemic and Narrative Work with Unaccompanied Asylum-Seeking Children

Stories of Relocation

Ana Draper, Elisa Marcellino, and Samantha Thomson

Routledge
Taylor & Francis Group

LONDON AND NEW YORK

Designed cover image: © Getty

First published 2024
by Routledge
4 Park Square, Milton Park, Abingdon, Oxon OX14 4RN

and by Routledge
605 Third Avenue, New York, NY 10158

Routledge is an imprint of the Taylor & Francis Group, an informa business

© 2024 Ana Draper, Elisa Marcellino, and Samantha Thomson

British Library Cataloguing-in-Publication Data
A catalogue record for this book is available from the British Library

ISBN HB: 978-1-032-19329-8
ISBN PB: 978-1-032-19331-1
ISBN EB: 978-1-003-25868-1

DOI: 10.4324/9781003258681

Typeset in Times New Roman
by Apex CoVantage, LLC

For those who dare to dream and hope.

Gratitude

This book would not have been possible without the generosity of the stories of young people and those professionals who have worked with them.

Thank you to our editors, Charlotte Burck and Gwyn Daniel, for their support, encouragement, and constant feedback. They have been alongside us on this journey, and we could not be more grateful for all they have done for us.

A thank you to Nina, our proofreader, who has patiently commented and directed us at times when the journey was unclear and difficult.

Our last thank-you goes to our families, who have been a consistent anchor in our lives during times of *Location, Dislocation, and Relocation.* They gave us strength and unconditional love. Their physical and spiritual presence has allowed an emotional nourishment that has enabled us to continue our bonds with them in what we shared on these pages.

Authors' biographies

Ana Draper: I am a consultant systemic psychotherapist and the systemic discipline lead for systemic psychotherapy at the Tavistock and Portman NHS Foundation Trust. I have obtained a doctorate in systemic psychotherapy and am also a clinical supervisor. Have worked in the fields of childhood bereavement and palliative care, with unaccompanied asylum-seeking children, as well as adopted and looked-after children. My current role is as outcomes lead, supporting the implementation of an all-systems change for Mindworks Surrey, a clinical alliance of which the Tavistock and Portman NHS Foundation Trust is a partner. I have written a number of research papers, as well as theory and practice links, and have presented my work in the United Kingdom, Ecuador, Malawi, Sierra Leone, Australia, and Europe. I have also received national awards for clinical excellence in a career that has spanned 30 years and given me the privilege of being with and learning from others.

Elisa Marcellino: I am a clinical, counselling, and health psychologist. I am currently training to become a psychodynamic psychotherapist. I can speak two languages fluently. Over the past years, I have gathered my experience in the National Health Service, local authorities, and the private sector in England. My specialist interests include attachments, relationships, complex trauma, adolescence, immigration, offending behaviour, bereavement, and neurodivergence. I am trained in different therapeutic approaches, including cognitive behavioural therapy (CBT), psychodynamics, narrative, acceptance and commitment therapy (ACT), mindfulness, and compassion. I am the co-author of several papers, including *Continuing Bonds Enquiry* and *Fast Feet Forward*. I have presented my work nationally and internationally, including with the European Family Therapy Association and the Association of Family Therapy in the UK.

Samantha Thomson: I am employed as a systemic psychotherapist and family therapist in South East London National Health Trust. I have over 25 years of experience working with adults, children, and families and have worked in many different settings. I am also a supervisor. My experience includes working in the National Health Service, charity, local authority, and education sectors, and I have specialised in working with previously looked-after children and unaccompanied asylum-seeking children. I have run parenting groups, including Non-Violent Resistance (NVR) and Family Connections. I have also delivered *Fast Feet Forward* groups with adopted children and asylum-seeking young people. My work has included training different professionals in the *Location, Dislocation, and Relocation* practice framework with both my colleagues and co-authors Ana and Elisa.

Contents

Series editors

We are delighted that this most timely book is being published in our series. Its overarching conceptual framework of location, dislocation, and relocation importantly addresses the most abiding questions of our contemporary world. Ana Draper, Elisa Marcellino and Samantha Thomson enter the world of dislocation through their experiences of working with unaccompanied asylum-seeking children and they engage us with the narratives of the children and young people using a finely tuned mixture of compassion, admiration and – above all – hope.

Providing stories of young people who describe their own ways of coping or giving advice to others embarking on their own journeys of relocation, the authors emphasise both agency and individual trajectories. This process is enhanced by the way the authors intersperse their professional writing with narratives of their own experiences of dislocation, transition, loss and challenge and emphasise the value both of appreciating diverse ways of responding to such challenges and the importance of seeking and finding connections between people.

This volume provides invaluable pointers to practice and shares a diverse range of frameworks for understanding the effects of the profound dislocations – familial, cultural, and societal – these young people have endured, frameworks which the authors have found translate well across the various disciplines involved with this work. In addition to their overarching systemic and narrative perspective, they draw upon trauma research, neuropsychology, physiology and attachment theory, always with a focus on moving beyond those bio-medical or individualised approaches to trauma, which can constrain the thinking of those who wish to help.

One unique feature of this volume is the attention paid to the often-misunderstood aspects of the experience of unaccompanied asylum-seeking children such as sleep and nutrition. These two chapters provide an invaluable guide for practitioners because they emphasise agency and an understanding that sleep or eating difficulties arise from the exigencies of harrowing journeys to safety and can be employed in practical ways that do not require revisiting these traumatic experiences.

From the range of interventions developed by the authors through their clinical action research, the *Fast Feet Forward* programme is one of the most impressive, embodying as it does a largely non-verbal approach and relying on kinetic activity using bilateral foot movements. The authors describe this work – embedded within a mind/body/emotions nexus – and share the processes of evaluation they have developed.

Throughout the book we not only learn the feedback of young people to the interventions developed, some of which they themselves contributed to, but also those of the other workers and interpreters involved in the programmes for young people. The book conveys a powerful sense of journeys made at many different levels: the young people as they attempt to relocate themselves within a new culture and to maintain continuing bonds with family members – alive or dead – that they have had to leave behind and the journeys made by the authors and other professional helpers as they travel alongside and learn more about hope, aspiration, and resilience.

We are proud to include this book in our series, which we think will provide a rich resource for all those engaged in this challenging work.

Charlotte Burck and Gwyn Daniel

Forward

Be prepared to be intrigued, sorrowed, and stimulated as you enter this heart-blistering and heart-healing book. Its format is a unique latticing of the courageous stories of young unaccompanied asylum seekers, the deeply committed therapist-authors who later accompany them, along with invitations to explore varied experiences with dislocation, relocation, sleep, trauma, food, distress, and resilience, including your own. Its pages are illumed with years of listening to and being in relationship with children who have grappled with loss and reconnection in multiple misplacements.

Whether you are a therapist, teacher, coach, psychologist, medical personnel, spiritual mentor, social worker, or in some other helping role, each chapter swirls you into vibrant conversations with clients, colleagues, and yourself. As well, the innovative strategies and ideas found in *Systemic and Narrative Work with Unaccompanied Asylum-Seeking Children* are informed by creative participatory research about support and accompaniment.

The young people at the centre of this book and those engaged with them are models of openness and curiosity for us all. As I read, admiration grew for Ana Draper, Elisa Marcellino, and Samantha Thomson, the three co-authors and their colleagues, Izzy, Kate, Nat, Martha, Johanne, Andy, Anna, Shona, Juan, Peter, Charlie, Rose, Laura, Stella, Ruth, Trish, Abrihat, Precious, Mateusz, Katie, Gill, and Melody. They ask hard questions with integrity, intricately examine themselves and their work, and unflinchingly reflect on things they need to shift and recalibrate. Furthermore, they probe with anger and passion the upheavals and legal limbos created for asylum seekers by our political and social service systems.

The United Nations High Commissioner for Refugees reports that a full 41% of people forcibly displaced by violence, human rights violations, environmental disasters, or other serious disturbances are children. As the number of youths traveling alone to seek asylum continues to rise, this volume is timely and essential.

I am profoundly grateful for the generative stories of the young asylum seekers quoted in each chapter: Alex, Danyal, Soul, Subin, Imad, Abel, Shila, Afri, Abram, Anil, Ordo, Assem, Lufti, Ahmed, Little Mo, Esmat, Fahad, Abul, Lidan, Timur, Suman, Saad, Basir, Girma, Parwan, Saab, Hamed, Carim, Aarash, Fariad, Jamal, Farci, Yar, Mohamed, Zahir, Able, Heidi, Feavan, Duka, Malik, Hussain, Damsa, Firash, Jennifer, Joseph, Jonathan, Najib, Fazal, Kione, Selassie, Yosief, Siddiq, Rose, Oman, and Safi.

These names are not the ones given to them by their families. To 'prevent fear of repercussions,' their given names have been changed. The co-authors went through a vibrant process to choose names for them. They thought about the character of each person and the 'wonder of them' and then looked for names from their country of origin with meanings that best captured them. And yet, the fact that the authors and the colleagues that they quote can use their real names underscores deep inequities.

In the future, may all the given names of these unaccompanied children be called, be known.

Janine Roberts, Professor Emerita,
University of Massachusetts, Amherst
7 September 2023 – Longview House, Leverett,
Massachusetts, USA

Life is a Journey

We start this book with a story. It is told by an unaccompanied asylum-seeking child, now an adult, to other children at a reception centre in Kent. This is his story, shared like a treasure map, guiding others at the beginning of their new journey.

There are further stories within this book, both from and about the children and young people we have worked with. We have chosen not to use any of their real names in order to prevent fear of repercussions. This is due to the often-negative connotations associated with the term *asylum-seeking* and the power differentials it invokes.

Alex's story: the journeys we make . . .

We are similar; you and I have shared situations, journeys and loss.
We have escaped with one beginning journey to a journey's end,
Just to start all over again.
So it is a beginning again and the journey is hard and long, similar and yet different.
This new journey is made step by step, it has many paths from which more loss can come,
And yet there are steps that take you to your dreams and hopes;
The dream of belonging, of safety, of freedom to be;
The dream that my kin will be safe and free.
In the beginning; at the start of the first journey, I turned to run from the massacre,
To escape the torture,
To run into your arms of safety.
And at that journey's end I was left naked of tongue, or knowing how to be,
I was left alone because of the fear in your eyes that spoke of my loss.
So I arrived, to start the journey again;
I arrived to a new place, a new culture and the socio-vertigo that made me dizzy
It put me into a spin.
I heard the stories that made the fear in your eyes,
I climbed the steps that made the fear go away.
I proved the lies of your fear to be untrue.
Each step a milestone; each step a victory.

DOI: 10.4324/9781003258681-1

Your lie said I would not speak, so I dived deep into your sounds and found I could make them,

Your lie said I would always take from you, so I learnt how I could earn and give you back more than you have given,

Your lie said that I would hurt you, so I learnt how to bring peace through a kaleidoscope of knowledge made up of the journeys, of education degrees and the socio-vertigo that I now understand and can translate.

Each step is a challenge; and the challenge is not the end of the world, it will change.

The challenge is never as bad as what you have seen and what could be;

In the moments of anger and fear, of not knowing, there are hands holding you, wishing you well.

Don't forget that you bring with you amazing things;

The stories our grandparents told us;

Our culture,

Our way of being community.

People here like to know these things, and it is a way we can contribute and give what is ours.

When I came and started this journey, I shared my music and the music made people look at me without fear and we became friends. The music is now something we share and celebrate together, it is us and our community, and we have all been changed.

What the Home Office decides, it does, what it does,

Yet in every other way you are in control;

So follow the steps, my steps, the steps of success, and the steps of doing and being your dreams.

I am a leader,

I am making a difference,

I am changing things,

My story is shared and told and retold – it honours my loss;

Yet my loss is never gone, it is in my breath, in my eyes, in my steps.

I am in a place of safety, and I can achieve.

Today is not my worst day;

Today I am held, and I hold you by sharing my steps to success.

> (As told to Ana, co-author, through her work with children
> and young people seeking asylum in Kent, 21 April 2016)

You will also notice that there are different voices in the stories that are told. These voices and their stories have enriched our knowledge and helped to shape our understanding. We want to thank all the people who have generously shared so much of their experience. We have also chosen to protect their identities in this book. They have been the fabric from which we have woven what we go on to describe in this book.

Chapter 1

Introduction to the framework

Starting with ourselves as co-authors

The three of us – Ana, Elisa, and Samantha – share our own stories of migration. We also share an interest in working with young people who have experienced multiple misplacements and losses; these include previously looked-after children, unaccompanied minors, and young offenders. In 2019, we decided to co-write this book to map out the journey we have made professionally and personally. Here are some of our personal stories of migration:

'I moved to England, aged nine, from Ecuador. I draw from all the experiences that Ecuador brings in terms of language, smells, relationships and food. The stories I tell are rooted in family and are a way of honouring them – my Uncle Fausto, my adopted sisters Angelita and Brendita. I also love to tell stories about rivers, tropical storms, and Uncle Sam, a Tsachila medicine man. I draw on the socio-vertigo I experienced (both in Ecuador as a British national and in England) as a child born and raised in Ecuador. I recall the moments of being socially and culturally different and the impact of this. All of these stories have expanded from one language to another, for example, from Spanish to English. They include the shift and change in the smells and the relationships and types of food eaten.'

(Ana, co-author)

'I was born and raised in the south of Italy, in a house with an incredible sea view. When I was 19 years old, I moved to Rome to study psychology. In 2015, I moved to the UK. Migration has been a significant theme in my life; it allowed me to notice the difference, more than the similarity, that comes with being a migrant. This has influenced my work and passion. Today, I like going to the seaside in England whenever I miss home. The sea and the smell of fish remind me of my hometown. I feel at home whenever I go there.'

(Elisa, co-author)

'I was born in Jersey and moved to Kent when I was five years old. I later moved to Scotland after qualifying as a family therapist. I lived there for 10 years. My identity grew from being a child in my birthplace to becoming an adult

DOI: 10.4324/9781003258681-2

with children somewhere else. Throughout my life, many events have shaped and reshaped my identity. I became a therapist, wife, and parent. Then things shifted; I moved back to Kent, bringing with me aspects of my past and present identities.'

(Samantha, co-author)

The three of us met for the first time in 2017 while working at an adoption service. Curiosity about each other and our work connected us. We were sparked by the idea that there is always more to learn and know.

'I used to sit near Ana and Samantha when we worked in the same office. We would welcome each other with a cup of coffee every morning, which made me feel at home. We also started a tradition of having pizza Fridays with more pizza than we could eat! When I changed jobs, they gave me a mug and coffee maker to take with me to the new office. It was a way of staying connected. A few days after I left, Samantha sent me a text saying she was using my old desk, as this reminded her of me.'

(Elisa, co-author)

Since that time, we have all moved jobs; we are no longer in the same workspace but rather are creating the space to remain connected. Our connection has been the delight of working together, of being together as more than colleagues, but rather transformed into friends.

'Ana and I were women at a similar stage in life. We had two older children going to university and two younger children who still required lots of support. We were able to see the humour in the antics that often took place in our personal lives, as well as the links we made to our work with families. We were also just generally grounded in the messiness of life.'

(Samantha, co-author)

Since then, much has changed. We have changed.

'I've ended up in a role that involves shaping a system with all the challenges it brings. I love the fact that Samantha and Elisa know me. They help me see that the madness in the system is something other than me. The intimacy of being known by them, I would say, is a key resource that keeps me going despite not always knowing how.'

(Ana, co-author)

This book is one of those challenges we were keen on taking together. It is a form of re-membering (membering again). It binds our life stories. It also brings together the stories and memories that we liken to pearls that have been gifted by others we have worked with. It is also a celebration of our friendship.

These stories and memories, collected throughout our lives, also include our family. Chapter after chapter, we have re-membered where we came from, the journey we have made, the challenges, the rewards, the laughter, and the tears. We also look back on the time spent with the young people we have worked with. The memory of their faces, voices, and the moments spent with them has flowed as we encouraged each other in the act of storytelling. These are stories we feel privileged to have been told and been a part of creating.

As our professional lives have grown, we have decided to share our thinking with others by attending systemic discipline conferences internationally and nationally. Fighting our fears and anxieties, we have spoken about our clinical work with young people in front of large audiences. We have written articles, continued working, and remain curious.

In this book, we are able to share the stories of those we have had the privilege to meet and walk alongside – and from where this map was made. Our passion, as in compassion (with passion), is to shape ways of 'being' and 'connecting' with children, young people, and their families, all of whom have had multiple adverse life experiences. We include them as part of a family because being unaccompanied does not mean they are not part of one.

Our learning in our work with children is shifting and changing. It is in a place of 'becoming' all of the time. Sometimes, we need to offer consultations, training, and supervision to others alongside this group of children, young people, and families. In doing this work, we have noticed how the system often reiterates a disadvantaged story (*dislocation*) and leaves untold the story of ability, hope, and strength (*location*). When this occurs, we notice that children, young people, and families are not supported with the resources and resilience to cope with and manage their situation (*relocation*). We, therefore, inadvertently further *dislocate* them. From here, our journey becomes a story of what we go on to term *Location, Dislocation, and Relocation*. It is a way of shaping and crafting the stories we tell – stories that are intertwined throughout the book.

This book aims to provide a contextualised understanding, derived from an Action Research project that I (Ana, co-author) was involved in 2016. The project looked at the emotional health and well-being of unaccompanied asylum-seeking children in Kent. This type of research is described as a step-by-step methodology in which the investigators(s) plan, act, observe, and reflect (Torbert, 2001). It is humanistic as it looks to work and collaborate with everyone who is involved and affected. It also helps us to explore emergent meaning and understanding with the young people we work with (Bland & Derobertis, 2019). The Action Research involved the project team, the staff at reception centres, social workers, non-governmental organisations, and unaccompanied asylum-seeking children in the observations and actions taking place. Therefore, all those involved, affected, and connected are an active part of the team and relational in nature. Bjorn (1996) and Shotter (1998) refer to participatory Action Research as a multi-dimensional, dialogical, and fluid form of self-development. It reflects Bateson's (1972) ideas that nothing is separate from anything else and that boundaries are limitless.

In observing the effect of our actions, at each stage of the cycle from which change emerges, we have been looking and will continue to look at building knowledge. This allows us to continuously incorporate findings into subsequent stages of our investigation. Our team has and will continue to change. For some, the journey has branched into other adventures. Others have recently joined the journey and bring a difference and new wondering to what can be. Yet the focus is always on the stories told by unaccompanied asylum-seeking children, young people, and their families. The book brings together the current evidence base for this new systemic and narrative practice framework of care.

The project in Kent found that the Action Research steps were a mirror of the process being undertaken in the interventions being developed, such as the sleep work. These interventions were responsive to the needs identified by unaccompanied minors in reception centres and the community.

The Migration Data Portal (2021), which provides information about migration statistics globally, confirms that unaccompanied asylum-seeking children are an international phenomenon. Practitioners, such as non-governmental organisations, nationalised social care services, and health care workers, are struggling to find ways to intervene effectively not only here in the UK but throughout the developed world, and especially through Europe and the United States. UNICEF (2015) states that 'the refugee and migrant crisis in Europe – whether off its coasts, on its shores, or along its roadsides – is a crisis for children.'

Alex, who tells his story in the introduction, has the lived experience of being an unaccompanied asylum-seeking child. He described what he called the 'steps to success,' and his story has informed the interventions being observed. In developing an understanding of what is needed, we created interlinking steps from which responses were collaboratively made. Therefore, unaccompanied asylum-seeking children are supported with a new understanding, formed from a practical, relational responsiveness to the stories they tell.

Unaccompanied minors, once they arrive in the host country, are interviewed to determine their refugee status. A review of the literature on unaccompanied minors' asylum claims reported that the decision-makers' personal experiences, beliefs, and emotional state contribute to and impact their decision-making procedure (Given-Wilson et al., 2016). Therefore, the authors suggested that a valid assessment of unaccompanied minors should take into consideration a multitude of factors (Given-Wilson et al., 2016). A subsequent review discussed what can be reasonably expected of an adolescent's autobiographical memory, especially when we consider the life journey of unaccompanied asylum-seeking children (Given-Wilson et al., 2017).

Izzy, a volunteer teacher and advocate from the reception centre in Kent, tells Danyal's story as follows:

'I'd heard that he'd run into difficulties with his asylum case. His solicitor had been a disaster, while the Home Office interrogator ridiculed him about his country of birth. "Can't you see Iran is over here, and Afghanistan is over there?" she said, rolling out a map and showing him both countries. She then questioned him further. "What were you doing in Mashhad, Iran?" Danyal then answered. "You'd have to ask my Mum; she was busy giving birth to me!!" Not everyone enjoys Danyal's sense of humour, and that was definitely not the right moment to make such a joke. "You're either stupid or a liar," the interrogator shouted back. That first question, "Where are you from?" was asked at two in the morning, wrongly placing Danyal in the Afghan box. It would take a long time for the truth to come to light and be accepted by those who asked the right questions. Those who eventually did, listened to his complex history and finally believed it.'

It is the same when the talk is about emotional health and well-being. The assumptions that are made, along with the interview style and lack of trust when yet another professional is asking questions, are likely barriers to what is heard and understood.

Izzy describes the effect of the right questions: the 'listening' and the 'believing.' These are supported by professionals who are persistent in challenging the dominant story of miscategorisation, as follows:

'The Home Office had accepted that Danyal was 'stateless.' He was given asylum. His solicitor was emotional and overwhelmed when Danyal had his asylum accepted for the first time. He later told me that it was the single most rewarding case he'd ever undertaken.

Danyal was overjoyed with the result. He told me he'd cried. I told him that we all cried, but they were tears of joy; we were all so happy for him. "Izzy, I owe you my life," Danyal said. "No, YOU did it." I replied. We learned how to fight together, and we did not give up.

On days like that, I appreciated what a privilege it was to play a part in helping such amazing young people.'

To avoid the barriers caused by assumptions, pre-knowledge, and beliefs, the project workers, including clinicians, were based near the reception centres. They became known to the boys as well as the staff. This enabled them to hear the different voices and to be curious about the stories told and the reason for telling them.

Here is a story of a conversation that took place during a training we were undertaking for a local authority.

'We noticed that the local authority was trying to enable staff to understand the children they were supporting. They did this by drawing a map of all the trauma and adverse childhood experiences a child had sustained. The intent was to ensure that the staff, who were caring for those young people, were able to make sense of some of the associated behaviours that came from those experiences. In the training session, we asked what stories had been mapped about other episodes and events that were not adverse. One of the attendees, a previously looked-after child (now an adult), told a story about his social worker. This social worker had said that if he wanted to have continued support from her and the system, he needed to ensure that he always had a prevailing and problem-saturated story to tell.'

(Elisa, co-author)

In order to work with this dilemma, we wanted to create for them the inter-determinacy between a sense of being *Located, Dislocated, and Relocated*, rather than just one description of the *dislocations* they had experienced. These descriptors encompass the idea of a journey. Many of the children, young people, and families we have worked with have experienced journeys that have *dislocated* them from the experiences and dangers they have faced and often continue to face. Yet, it does not define them to a single description but amplifies other descriptions and stories that are theirs and often remain unknown and untold.

This way of thinking and the opportunities it crafts have increased our need to tell these stories. It also makes connections, in the junctures of our understanding, about the 'difference that makes a difference' in how care can be delivered to this large and continually expanding cohort of children, young people, and families. These needs require a system-wide approach, from which change can come. The overwhelming task of change, from which transformation is possible, can result in professionals feeling frozen in their thinking. We need to think about how and what to offer to support a child or young person's journey of physical and emotional well-being.

What the map tells us and the current context

Due to the current and ongoing refugee crisis and the increase in the number of unaccompanied children seeking asylum, there is a need to develop a governance and early intervention framework. This will support the quality of care with respect to the emotional health and well-being interventions that can be delivered.

This work is pertinent to us all, wherever we are *located*, due to the practice of the dispersal of these children to many geographical localities. As co-authors, we have woven together our different life experiences, different cultures, and different ways of being. This is so that we can continue on this journey with the combined known resources and abilities that hold us together. Our differences have shaped our curiosity. These 'wondering' questions (Draper & Hannah, 2008) have supported us in bringing together a collection of ideas. This collection of ideas has shaped and continues to mould a framework of interventions that, we hope, can bring positive change to the landscape of work with unaccompanied asylum-seeking children.

We invite you to join us so we can continue to develop innovative practices with this sometimes forgotten and neglected group of children, young people, and their families.

At the centre of this book is the practice framework we have named *Location, Dislocation, and Relocation*. It explains the experiences of unaccompanied asylum-seeking children, young people, and families, along with the stories that their journeys have created. The thinking, the stories, and the meaning, together with how we have applied them, are explained in Chapter 2. The book also includes protocols used to support well-being and resilience-based support, such as the *Distress Screening Tool* (described in Chapter 4), *Sleep Work* (in Chapter 5), *Nutrition Work* (Chapter 6), *Continuing Bonds Enquiry* (in Chapter 7), and *Fast Feet Forward* (in Chapter 8). In Chapter 3, the impact of adverse life experiences on the brain is described. In Chapter 9, we reflect on the framework and our journey so far.

The framework aims to create a wider understanding of working with trauma responses in unaccompanied asylum-seeking children. It offers coherence for practitioners wanting to use this approach. It also supports the ability of a common language to be used, one that is multi-disciplinary and has the potential to create coordination and excellence in care abilities within the whole system.

The book will, therefore, be of interest to (and is aimed primarily at) practitioners working with this clientele. It is also for students of psychology, social work, and other mental health disciplines who will dedicate some part of their lives to this population. It will also be of interest to policymakers and political thinkers to foreground the needs of this community so that they can provide more adequate services. Additionally, it may provide ideas for international practitioners working with this clientele, including non-governmental organisations, health services, and social service practitioners who are struggling to find ways to support and enable them in effective ways throughout the developed world, especially throughout Europe and the USA.

And so the stories are told as the journey begins

Let us introduce you to a young boy named Soul, whom I (Ana, co-author) met after he settled into a new home environment. He had been in the UK for several years. Soul shared his story with me (Ana, co-author), and the excerpts appear throughout this chapter.

> 'Soul talked about being an asylum seeker but wanting to become a refugee. His hands would shake as he picked up the post in case a decision letter arrived that could instantly change his world. A few words, written as if they were nothing – "application granted," "application denied" – exploding like a bomb of happiness, fear, or both. Soul cried; he laughed and cried again. Application granted! He had become a refugee for the time being.'

The displacement of minors, such as Soul, is part of a worldwide crisis that provokes extreme political and emotional reactions. These can be witnessed by monitoring the language of some media. There is a widespread confusion of attitudes and knowledge about what is possible. This is compounded by a conflation of the notion of 'immigration' with the territory of what it means to be a refugee and an asylum seeker. The political volatility of this crisis cannot be disregarded. There is a moral and humanitarian obligation to look urgently past the rhetoric and into the reality of what is happening. The health needs of this vulnerable group of children require the devising of operational strategies, as well as further research and a national and worldwide response.

Unaccompanied asylum-seeking children are young people, under the age of 18, who travel without a parent or caregiver. Asylum seekers are different from refugees in that they seek international protection. This is due to the fact that their refugee status has yet to be decided. This also makes them different from other immigrants who might leave their homes voluntarily (Rehn-Mendoza, 2020).

All unaccompanied minors, whether they seek asylum or not, are entitled under international law to special protection (Rehn-Mendoza, 2020). The United Nations Convention on the Rights of the Child (2019) is a primary convention that governs the treatment of unaccompanied minors and acknowledges the importance of their rights. It clearly enforces that every child should be protected, respected, and recognised.

'Soul spoke about the lorry in which he had travelled. The hiding, the cold, the fear of harm, as he clung onto items in the lorry for dear life. In the journey he had made across Europe, he was chased, beaten, and worked on fishing boats to have enough money for food and warm clothes. He had settled at a port in France, looking for lorries in which he could stow and reach his promised land, where a distant relative lived. There was no safe passage; there was no legal route; there was just the gaggle of friends he had made along the way. They had become kin as the journey progressed. They protected each other, they recognised each other, and they respected their differences and similarities, holding each other as they sought to gain asylum in a safe place.'

These young people often travel as a consequence of traumatic experiences in their native country. In addition, they have often endured dangerous and difficult journeys. These have sometimes involved trafficking, violence, abuse, detention in other countries, and multiple forms of exploitation and persecution. As Soul mentioned, often these young people semi-starve for weeks or even months. We discuss semi-starvation and nutrition tools in Chapter 6.

'Soul talked about hurting his leg while trying to escape a prison in Syria. He dropped from a high building as he jumped to escape the soldiers. He talked about the torture, the beatings, and running with his leg throbbing. His ability to run some of the fastest times in the world is inconsequential when running for his life. This was a different type of race – a race with a price. A race with only one goal – to be safe, to be alive, and to arrive at a place he could call home.'

The Department for Education (2019) reported that 90% of unaccompanied asylum-seeking children were males and 85% were over the age of 16, while 87%

cited their primary needs as an absent parent. The main countries of origin where unaccompanied asylum-seeking children have journeyed include Afghanistan, Sudan, the Arab Republic, Syria, Eritrea, and Iraq. The majority of unaccompanied asylum-seeking female children come from Eritrea (Dansokho, 2016).

There is international recognition that unaccompanied asylum-seeking children are highly vulnerable. The number of refugees around the world amounts to 26 million globally (Amnesty International, 2021). This is an ever-increasing number, given the global instability of so many countries. The number of unaccompanied children migrating has increased in the past few years. In 2020 alone, there were an estimated 14.6 million new displacements of children globally (UNICEF, 2021). This trend of increased child immigration is likely to continue over the next few years.

'Soul talks about his fear that his sister will also make the journey he has made. The fear of what will happen to her, the fear that she will be raped. He wants to stop her from making the same journey. He wants to protect her from the things he has experienced. He wants safe passage for her. Yet he knows there is nothing he can do. She needs to leave behind the world that is her home. It is no longer safe for her to be there. It is no longer home. It is a place of danger and violence, a place where she needs to hide her skills and abilities and become invisible. Yet, the visibility created in the journey she is about to make means she is a target. She is vulnerable to those with power and those who abuse that power and can choose to use her like a slave.'

The distress experienced is compounded due to multiple transitions being made because of the migration trajectory. This includes moving to a novel socio-economic system, creating a shift from their own culture to a foreign one with the need to learn a new language (Bhugra, 2004). These experiences are frequently followed by a culture shock, otherwise described as 'socio-vertigo,' due to the differences between the native and new cultures (Alhawsaw, 2016). This includes exposure to cultural barriers where immigrants try to build a new identity in the host country (Alhawsaw, 2016).

'Soul feels the crisis. He has been and remains in crisis. The homecoming he had hoped for – the sense of belonging and safety – dissipated. His anxiety rises with the thought of his sister. His own socio-vertigo returns as he tries to understand this whole new world with all its customs, rules, and ways of being. This is not his own known way, not his known humour or laughter, not his ease in spirit. He feels like he is being made to walk in another man's shoes in this strange land with its jarring sounds and weather. The knife and fork in his hands remind him that he is a stranger in a strange land.'

Children and young people like Soul and his sister are extremely vulnerable to experiencing trauma before, during, and after migration. This is due to the substantial challenges faced throughout the migratory journey (Nemoyer et al., 2019). Sandahl et al. (2013) discuss the three faces of traumatic events that can represent the precursors of mental health illness in these young people. These are exposure to events in their home country, neglect and assault during the journey, and a prolonged post-migration stay in reception centres. The latter is often followed by multiple placements, a lack of social contact, and cultural isolation.

'It is the third time now that his social worker has left their role. The person Soul starts to trust who disappears to be replaced by another. He had been so keen to leave the reception centre and to have a place he could call home. Yet he discovered that home was a place of isolation, a place where he needed to learn a whole new way of survival. He started to travel to attend a church in London, where his language was present and the sacred rituals and fasting were understood. There were people like him, their faces mirroring his own. When they ate the food of home together, it was with fingers, and they all knew the rules and how to feed together as a community. It was a glimmer of home, a locating place where, for that time each week, he could feel safe with the familiarity of the past.'

Often, part of the post-migration phase can involve temporary settlement before resulting in the final resettlement experience. These experiences are also impacted by the prolonged separation from caregivers, those who migrated earlier, and those who were left behind (Nemoyer et al., 2019).

During each of these journeys, unaccompanied minors face multiple physical, physiological, and social challenges (Dansokho, 2016). Sleep issues are experienced as a recurring feature for unaccompanied children. There are reports of a lack of sleep and disturbed sleep, often turning night into day (Carr et al., 2017). In Chapter 5, sleep deprivation, its impact, and sleep work are discussed.

Pre-migration

The reasons why people migrate often depend on their country of origin's social and cultural background. It also depends on personal or familial aspirations. In most cases of child migration, the immediate and structural causes are closely interconnected (Human Rights Council, 2016).

There are often different motivations for why some migrant young people apply for asylum and others do not. Those children who do not apply for asylum are often moved by the desire to have a better future. Once in the host country, these children do not always want to be registered or cared for in reception centres. This limits the information available on them (Human Rights Council, 2016).

The migrant children who do apply for asylum often leave their home country because of a generalised state of violence or due to fear of persecution (Human Rights Council, 2016). In these circumstances, the experience of trauma is triangulated for these children in that they have run from their homeland due to adverse circumstances. Some of these include escaping violence, domestic violence or sexual abuse, kidnappings, and economic deprivation (Valdez et al., 2015).

'Soul had left his mother and sister. They had encouraged him to leave. He was reaching an age where he would be forced to join the army, with all the dangers of war thrown in. Soul talks about his father, who had also been recruited into the army long before Soul was born. He talks about the rare visits when his father would come home. These visits were always unexpected. The length of time they spent together varied and was always unknown. He remembers his father weeping at the idea of Soul having the same life as him. His biggest regret was that he didn't get away when he could have. He implores Soul to run from being forced to kill or be killed. To run from being forced to fight a war that no one wants or believes in and to die in an unknown place with unknown people.'

The literature indicates that the primary reason motivating people to leave their homes comes down to child recruitment into gangs, gender-based violence, extortion, and war (Jones & Podkul, 2012). The lack of a solid economic system and education opportunities are contributing factors to this violence (Vogt, 2013). The separation from their parents due to the immigration process can cause a young person to experience significant distress. This can include depression and other emotional and behavioural difficulties (Heymann et al., 2009; Suárez-Orozco et al., 2002).

'Yet, at the time, Soul asked himself, how could he leave his sister and his mother? How could he walk away from them and leave them unprotected? What would happen to them once it became known that he had run? How could he leave the town where he was born and the small job he had in his aunt's shop? Who would mend the chairs and things that got broken at home? How could he leave behind his running coach? The fast times that were his and were on records that were known around the world. He tried to hold on to and treasure the dream of being like Bolt, the fastest man on the planet. Yet the journey took that from him. His leg was no longer able to support the explosive muscle power needed due to scar tissue.'

During migration

The journey itself is also unsafe and consists of crossing multiple borders through different means of transport. This can include buses, boats, and cars, all over a period of months.

In addition to experiencing violence in their home country, migration also exposes young people to additional trauma through the experience of abuse while on the journey (Valdez et al., 2015). Also, children immigrating have fewer social resources to enhance their resilience. They are particularly vulnerable to victimisation during the migration journey (DeLuca et al., 2010).

> 'The images that come to mind when Soul thinks about his sister making the journey are real. They are what he has seen and witnessed; they are his own experiences of violence and rape on the journey he has made. They are real in his own loss of naivety, the loss of being protected, and the loss of being held by his family and community. Soul knows that loss; he knows that it is something he never wants another human being to experience, especially his sister. The distress is very present. He can't protect her, and he can't stop what might happen. His anxiety rises at the memories and what they might mean for her.'

Studies support the reality of Soul's experience and fear by highlighting the abuse, police brutality, extortion, rape, dismemberment, and death experienced by immigrants (Valdez et al., 2015). Some immigrants have reported witnessing sexual violence, robbery, and assault throughout their journey (Valdez et al., 2015). In Chapter 8, we will discuss an early intervention protocol that supports young people's well-being after they have experienced multiple traumas.

Post-migration

On arrival in the host country, unaccompanied asylum-seeking children face further questions of legitimacy, age assessments, and the prolonged uncertainty of gaining asylum.

Unaccompanied children have little sense of what awaits them when they arrive in their country of resettlement. Often, expectations are increased in hopes of less hardship. There is also a prominent belief that they will be given safety in a respectful and dignified manner. However, this is often compromised when a country that is designated as safe, privileging human rights as a basic requirement, creates multiple hurdles that reduce an unaccompanied minor's feeling of stability (Nardone & Correa-Velez, 2016).

Contributing factors that influence this position are immigration policies and their processes for claiming asylum status and leave to stay. Also, there are the prejudices and hostility of the resettlement country. These can be exhibited by members of a racial group towards those seeking asylum (Nardone & Correa-Velez, 2016; Masocha & Simpson, 2012). There has been considerable emphasis, based on public perception, that this cohort of young people will place unprecedented pressure and strain on a country's finances and resources (English & Mann, 2021). They are perceived as a 'social problem.' This is driven by a media focus suggesting that unaccompanied minors can have a negative influence on society. These additional factors contribute to the migration phase, creating further vulnerability and disadvantage.

> 'Soul's social worker had helped him to have legal representation, as there were lots of questions being asked about his age. Was he really 17 or older? When

Soul met with the Home Office, they kept asking about his age. Yet, at last, they seemed to understand that he left home at a certain age because it caused him to be at risk. He felt that his story was being questioned, that he was not believed, and that those around him felt he was being dishonest and didn't merit their protection. Each time he had to go to the Home Office, he became anxious. His ability to speak and tell his story was compromised. Soul didn't understand how important that arbitrary age cut-off was. Yet it seemed so important to those around him. He felt anxious, confused, scared, unheard, and vulnerable. This was not a safe place. This was a place where he was becoming more and more displaced.'

The loss of the native culture's elements, such as language, values, families, native songs, familiar food, and traditions, becomes part of the immigration trajectory (Henry et al., 2005; Akhtar, 2001). In Chapter 7, grief and loss will be explored by looking at *Continuing Bonds* as a form of *Enquiry*.

'We were doing an assessment when Subin told me, "I can't speak English. How can I ever change my life here in the UK? How can I find a job?" My mind sifted through my last few years in the UK, my decision to move to London, the difficulties with the language, and building a life here. In those few seconds, everything moved in a time lapse. I saw myself and how different my life was just before this job. Wow! How much energy it took for me to achieve this – to be here as a psychologist working in the National Health Service. So I shared my journey of learning English and the challenges of working with this new language. I wanted him to know that it was and is possible. He looked at me, unsure of what to say, then kindly smiled and said, "Thank you."'

(Elisa, co-author)

Subin and I (Elisa, co-author) had multiple social differences (e.g. gender, ethnicity, race, education, religion, and class). The privileges of these elements were visible in our countries of origin. However, immigration made these elements of privilege less recognised in the UK. Here, we were both 'immigrants' with an accent, foreign qualifications, and a Mediterranean appearance. I (Elisa, co-author) wanted Subin to recognise that there were similarities in our journey, regardless of the privileges I might have had.

Additionally, it is important to note that the age limit of 18, present in some western countries, is not a worldwide standard. Often, this age limit does not correspond with the young refugee's culture, where a strict separation between child and adult does not exist. Therefore, it could occur that an unaccompanied minor may have left their country as an adult and be considered a child in Europe (Derluyn & Broekaert, 2007).

The loss of social status and significant relationships is also a part of the journey, along with many other changes, experienced when immigration takes place (Yaglom, 1993). A study completed by Valdez et al. (2015) highlighted how migrating families are characterised by structural vulnerability (Quesada et al., 2011). This vulnerability is defined as an inequality resulting from systemic political, economic, and material marginalisation. It further contributes to oppression through gender, ethnic, and class-based discrimination (Quesada et al., 2011).

As a result of this, unaccompanied young people are more likely to experience traumatic stress reactions compared to those who arrive with a family member (Bean et al., 2007). Montgomery & Foldspang (2001) found that family environments and feelings of safety, provided by a parental presence, were modifying factors of sleep disturbance in refugee children. The difficult living situation that an unaccompanied minor experiences is highly likely to affect their emotional well-being. This, in turn, can result in emotional and behavioural difficulties (Fazel et al., 2012). The uncertainty experienced can often make these young people, at times, rightly believe that it will be difficult to realise their dreams. This may cause conflicts of loyalty towards their families and home countries, to which promises may have been made (Derluyn & Broekaert, 2007). Family honour is the highest aim in family-oriented cultures compared with individually-oriented cultures (Pinto, 2007). It indicates a crucial cultural difference between western countries and separated young people.

> 'Soul wanted to realise his dream of being a runner. His hope of being the best. He wanted to achieve what he was on the way to becoming before he left his homeland. Now this identity is shattering and slipping away from him.'

Distress and its impact on young people's well-being are addressed further in Chapter 4, where the *Distress Screening Tool* will be presented.

The clinical picture

It is important to consider an individual's psychological well-being as they experience multiple losses and *dislocations*. These will all have an inevitable effect on their sense of self (Hughes & Rees, 2016). Unaccompanied minors are reported to have high levels of post-traumatic stress disorder symptoms. They are also reported to have high exposure to maltreatment (both sexual and physical) and high levels of anxiety in comparison to their host peers and refugees who emigrated and were accompanied (Bean et al., 2007). A study of Central American refugee children revealed that 30% had post-traumatic stress disorder (Betancourt et al., 2012). Also, these young people are reported to have high levels of anxiety and depression (Derlyun & Broekaert, 2007; Sourander, 1998). Montgomery's (1998) research reported that two-thirds of refugee children were clinically anxious. The most frequently reported symptoms of anxiety were 'fear of sleeping without light,' 'fear of being alone,' and 'clinging to parents.'

Furthermore, these young people generally meet the diagnosis criteria for major depressive disorder, agoraphobia, and generalised anxiety disorder (Jakobsen et al., 2014). There is also a higher risk of suicide with these young people, more so than with their counterparts (Hagström et al., 2018). We have highlighted four key themes that have emerged from their clinical work with unaccompanied minors (Draper & Marcellino, 2020). These key themes include the following: disordered sleep patterns, semi-starvation, hopelessness, and multiple traumas. The impact of these adverse life experiences on young people's brains and behaviours will be further described and addressed in Chapter 3.

Trauma and distress can become embodied within the self due to experiences held within the body, mind, and heart. When such emotions are repressed and unprocessed, it can lead to chronic physical and emotional health difficulties connected to our well-being. The use of the sleep and nutrition protocols in Chapters 5 and 6, together with the *Fast Feet Forward* intervention in Chapter 8, shows the importance of integrating body awareness into the clinical process. It does this by creating awareness of inner physical sensations and allowing the release of bodily tensions, the carriers of traumatic memory (Levine, 2010).

'A person is the sum total of his life experience, each of which is registered in his personality and structured in his body' (Lowen, 1994). In his book, Lowen discussed the importance of understanding how our body functions energetically. This energy determines what we feel, think, and do. Whenever an event occurs in the external world, one experiences its impact on the body rather than just experiencing it as an emotional conflict. For instance, for those who experience depression and trauma, there is often a lack of energy. This is the result of chronic muscular tensions due to a condition caused by the suppression of feelings. The body is linked to and connected to experience, and it responds accordingly. It won't always respond in the same way, as the response is contextual, individual, and connected to other relational experiences. We cannot assume a certain type of response, yet we should be curious about the body and what it is telling us about the young person's experience.

'I first met Imad at a reception centre in Kent, where I was a volunteer teacher. A social worker brought him to sit at my table and explained that he had arrived overnight. Imad was visibly shaking and breathing erratically. His head was down, and his hands covered his face. I laid my hand on his shoulder. Another Hazara boy arrived and sat beside him, translating the lesson into Dari. Still, Imad didn't look up, although his trembling grew less. During the break, I asked the same Hazara boy to ask the name of this new arrival. When Imad tried to speak, I realised he had such a bad stutter that he was not able to utter a single word.'

(Izzy, a volunteer teacher and advocate)

The emotional health and well-being needs, as well as the protection and best interests of each one of these children, should always come first. It is a matter that touches our principles as a humane society and our embedded responsibility. Children are victims of humanitarian crises; they are not the cause of them. Many of these young people would need access to diagnosis and treatment, as well as early intervention programmes, upon their arrival in the host country.

Social workers, non-governmental organisations, support workers, and other systems around separated young people are complex and diverse. Each agency is governed by Article 12 of the UNCRC (2019) and should work towards a child's best interest in the processes and decisions being undertaken. Yet each has a different role and relationship with the child, which can, at times, be problematic. There are also statutory rights that come into play. These can be challenging due to capacity and resource constraints. Each agency has its own governance structures, which often do not overlap. An agreement about what each understands, when considering an unaccompanied minor's emotional health and well-being, should be considered so that clinical excellence and capacity issues can be regulated. To enable this to happen, interactions between agencies are key. This will be further explored in Chapter 9.

White (2002) and Myerhoff (1982) discussed being an outsider witness to the stories lived and told. This connects to Tauvon (1998)'s ideas of everyone having the ability to see through another person's eyes. The primary element of transformation for an individual is to have the experience to witness themselves (Tauvon, 1998). Therefore, at the end of each chapter, we will be inviting you to be the audience for the stories and links we have made.

Izzy, the volunteer teacher and advocate who we introduced earlier, describes it as follows:

'To some, the word 'refugee' is just a word, but, to me, it is a hundred faces and so many untold case histories. The Native American aphorism tells us that if we truly wish to understand someone, we need to 'walk a mile in their shoes.' There are times in life when we have to acknowledge that things we've seen cannot be unseen. Neither can the things we've heard go unheard. All we can do is bear witness to all we've seen and heard.'

We will use Outsider Witness as a process, which has three stages (Walther & Fox, 2012) as follows:

- Each chapter is a telling of the story, with us as the tellers.
- There is an invitation to retell the story to yourself, using the 'sense-making' you have made.
- Finally, there is the retelling of the retelling, where we hear all our stories echoed in what you (as an individual) go on to create.

Outsider Witness reflection notes you may want to make about Chapter 1 are as follows:

- What connected me to these stories?
- What 'sense' do I make of these stories, and how do they align with who I am?
- How do I feel in my skin when witnessing these stories?
- How quickly or slowly did I read?
- Where does my mind take me, and what does it link me to?
- How will I retell my story to those I work with?
- How will this change what I might, or might not, do next?

Chapter 2

Location, Dislocation, and Relocation

We have heard John Burnham say, 'Be interested in what repulses you.' And so in our repulsion, we began to become interested in the impact of trauma on behaviours at a personal and corporate level. We began to play with words and developed a different language that shaped our thinking about trauma. This is when we started to use the framework of *Location, Dislocation, and Relocation*. We noticed we were in a relational process of learning as we joined one another with different experiences and knowledge. There were various theoretical frameworks (e.g. Bateson, 1964; Watzlawick, 1964; Ziminski, 2017) that underpinned our ethics and values in drawing upon this new framework. We will go on to describe it further in this chapter.

> 'Trauma in a person, decontextualised over time, looks like personality. Trauma in a family, decontextualised over time, looks like family traits. Trauma in people, decontextualised over time, looks like culture.'
>
> (Resmaa Menakem)

Overarching theoretical frameworks

The Approach-Method-Technique (Burnham, 1992) is a way to create coherence when we differentiate between types of activities and how these might be viewed. It helps us to identify and understand the movement between informed approaches that are taken, including the methods and techniques within that approach. This links to the connections that can be made, both in theory and practice. Within systemic psychotherapy, there has been an evolution of understanding, coming from influences and associations that have informed the approach that has been taken. An example of this evolution is seen in the historical development of systemic therapy, which has been influenced by the works of Milan (Palazzoli, Boscolo), Post-Milan (Checchin, Boscolo, Campbell), Attachment Narrative (Bowlby), Conversational (Anderson), Coordinated Management of Meaning (Pearce, Cronen, Cooperrider, Whitney), Narrative (White, Epston), and Dialogical (Shotter, Seikkula). Even Burnham's Approach-Method-Technique has had many and varied influences where he *locates* meaning as something derived from a context. In doing this, he shaped the idea that

DOI: 10.4324/9781003258681-3

context and meaning are acting in a recursive relationship with one another. This is linked to the Coordinated Management of Meaning theory, from which there is an understanding that stories emerge and meaning is made in the coordination of the communication that is taking place. Stories are fluid and are evolving in the process of interactions (Pearce & Cronen, 1980; Pearce & Pearce, 2004).

Narrative and social constructionist theory from which the Location, Dislocation, and Relocation practice framework emerged

Gergen (1985) defines social constructionism as the influence of social and inter-personal aspects in one's life. In migratory communities, these influences can be linked to *dislocation* by defining the individual and the community. The dominant story of who someone is and what they can do is not just based on their migratory history. These young people are linked to social settings that are geographically shaped by the terrain they are in at any given time. They are on the move, and the interpersonal aspects of their lives are defined by others. What is their age? What is their gender? Where have they come from? What is their DNA? They are 'aliens,' and they are placed as being 'the other' in the process of seeking asylum.

> 'My parents named me as a way of honouring an aspect of my identity as a Quit-enia from Ecuador. In my first week at a British primary school, my new teacher asked me to write my name. I duly wrote 'A N A'. My teacher looked at what I had written and exclaimed, "Oh my God! She doesn't even know how to spell her name." It was the 'even' that struck me. What had I done wrong?'
>
> (Ana, co-author)

We described how interpersonal stories of family life (e.g. spiritual and cultural experiences as well as families' hopes and expectations) can emerge in the present as opportunities and resources (Draper et al., 2022). Added to this, Kohli (2011) asserted that by relying on the retained affiliations from the past, unaccompanied minors can cope in the present. Mental well-being is improved once there is a sense of belonging to the country of origin and the host country (Straiton et al., 2019). Therefore, adopting the new country's language and behaviours while maintaining their own ethnic identity is fundamental (Rehn-Mendoza, 2020).

Alex, whose story we shared at the beginning of Chapter 1, points to this narra-tive. Our own experiences of migration also show this.

> 'There are days when I miss speaking Italian, as my entire day is filled with words and sounds that have become familiar to me, yet they are not entirely familiar. When I can, at the weekend, I like meeting with my friends who belong to the same community. This brings a sense of home. The feeling of being an Italian in the UK.'
>
> (Elisa, co-author)

By only mapping our inner conversations, which are based on adverse situations, we are limiting our ability to give voice to the positive, alternative narratives of the life we have lived. The 'traumatised child,' the 'asylum seeker,' the 'uneducated,' etc. This consequently limits our ability to speak about our competencies, beliefs, values, and skills, as our and other people's narratives are clouded by the traumatic experience. In evaluating alternative stories, we enable young people to scrutinise their relationship with the difficulties in their lives. We enter a process with them that is about lessening the impact of problems because they can develop access to alternatives that are about resources and abilities (Bruszt & Stark, 2003). This allows difficulties to be externalised in a process in which the dominant discourse is weakened and the preferred story is strengthened (White & Epston, 1990).

'On that cold morning in early April 2020, the news filled the main national journals. Stories of people who seemed destined to end their lives in the cold solitude of a hospital bed. Everything seemed to move in a chilling time lapse, under the rain, where everyone, or almost everyone, had stopped paying attention. The rain had always been there; it marked the rhythms of the lives of the millions of people who crowded London. Those people who had walked on its streets and lived in those terraced houses – just a few weeks ago, I was among those people. On that day, nobody was on those streets, and I was in my home working while the world out there was changing due to the Covid pandemic.'

(Elisa, co-author)

A narrative approach invites us to see our inner conversations from different perspectives. Deconstructive Questioning (Freedman & Combs, 1996) is used to create a more effective and helpful narrative and aims to empower oneself. Yet, meaning emerges in the process of relating, and it is constructed during the back and forth between people in conversation and communication (Cronen, 1994; Cronen et al., 1988; Pearce, 1994). The focus is on what meaning was being made during the turns that are crafted through the conversations and episodes (Cronen, 1994; Cronen et al., 1988; Pearce, 1994).

'When I got home, I asked my mum and dad how to spell my name. Did I get it right? Did it need to change? They were clear that my name is Ana and that they would speak to my teacher to ensure that he got it right in the future.'

(Ana, co-author)

Pearce (1994) first introduced the idea that, in communication, it is important to notice the interactions. This is where perspectives, practices, and the effects of those perspectives and interactions are brought together and understood. The Coordinated Management of Meaning highlights how meaning is context dependent. There are episodes and speech acts embedded in multiple contexts. These contexts include, but are not limited to, how we see ourselves, our relationships with others, and our identification within a given group.

It also includes the rules we construct for a particular episode with the culture, life scripts, and so on (Cronen et al., 1988; Pearce, 2001, 2004). Pearce (1994) described inter-relational responses as a graphical representation where we see positive changes made. These positive changes are concentrated in a small space and lie at the centre of the nucleus. He defined this as an atomic model. This enables the viewer to see interdependent relationships, how they shift and change, and what they create in their coming together.

These meanings create stories. Yet, stories are not linear or fixed in a certain type of telling; they are evolving. Not all stories are equal, and to support a way of *locating* and describing the different types, the Coordinated Management of Meaning can be used as an approach to amplify and prioritise them. This approach highlights how stories can be lived, whereas other stories remain untold, unknown, or even unheard. Yet, once they are explored, they can expand a collective and individual understanding of where the story fits in relation to oneself and others. So, in the collective act of telling, the untold story becomes known and told.

As the approach has become widely used, it has been shortened to the acronym LUUUTT (Pearce & Pearce, 1990). Yet, like all approaches, there has been an expansion, with the addition of undigested stories that further link to the *Location, Dislocation, and Relocation* framework. Undigested stories can be associated with an embodied experience. This embodied experience is then embedded in an episode or speech act and can also include 'difficult to digest' stories (Pearce & Pearce, 1990; Johnston & Robinson, 2017).

'When Elisa and I first met through work, it was around Christmas time. The office was decorated with lights and trees, and everything looked very festive. I asked Elisa some curious questions about how she would celebrate Christmas in her home country and what food she would have on the day. Elisa spoke about having a big dinner on the 24th of December that included eating a fish course. She then asked me what I would have as the main course. I spoke about a traditional English turkey dinner. Elisa responded, "What is a turkey?" Because we didn't know each other well at that point, we shared stories of ourselves and our own culture. These stories, although familiar from our own cultures, were untold stories within our relationship. Therefore, these stories became told, known, and shared.'

(Samantha, co-author)

Geography as a way to understand stories

In listening to the young people's stories we realised that geography is an important context in which we understand ourselves. The relationship between a place and self has a reciprocal influence. There is no place without self and vice versa (Casey, 2001).

The other day, in a teaching session, Ana told a story about herself as follows:

'At my school, you sat at the back of the class, not to be naughty but rather to avoid the chair flying through the air as the lesson took place. It was the school at the edge of the town, the comprehensive school, where only failures and misfits went. If you wanted to be successful and achieve, you had to go to the school in the middle of the small market town – the grammar school. It was seen as a centre of pride by the community, with the local vicar taking services at the school and being an active part in the school's life. He never came to my school. Maybe it was the flying chairs that stopped him?'

(Ana, co-author)

In this story, Ana, co-author, used language to describe the different schools, such as 'comprehensive' or 'grammar.' When asked to explain more, Ana thickened the story by saying that the *location* of the schools was about belonging or not belonging. One school was like a cathedral with a theatre, boarding houses, and a record number of entrants to Oxford or Cambridge. The other was a 1970s build, ramshackle and uninviting. It was like the council estate, a place that should be hidden from sight.

This story is an example of a type of map created for an individual by the virtue of the school they attended. It also includes the meanings and beliefs that are shaped and formed as a result of this. Furthermore, it represents the loss of possibilities and futures that are embedded in such a terrain – the 'being' in a local comprehensive school when there is a grammar school nearby.

Sometimes, places are viewed with a description as a fixed map. The framework explores *location* using a more open and extended meaning. It becomes a process rather than a fixed position. *Location* becomes connected to other places and cultural, historical, economic, and political influences.

Our experience as clinicians is that the *Location, Dislocation, and Relocation* as a practice framework (Draper & Marcellino, 2023a, 2023b) can be used as an early intervention. It uses geographical descriptors to create the inter-determinacy between a sense of being *located, dislocated*, and *relocated* – at any part of the journey. It is not about making a diagnosis, but rather it aims to create a common language that can be used in a multi-disciplinary and agency context. It has the potential to increase coherence, coordination, and care abilities within the system. An example of this might be when a young person is in transition between different homes. The local authority, education, and non-governmental organisations can then have greater common awareness of the increased vulnerability and distress of the young person. A solution-focused process that is embedded in the *Distress Screening Tool* allows shared decision-making that supports distress reduction. This tool will be further described in Chapter 4.

This framework aims to provide a new lens for seeing and understanding trauma. In the Diagnostic and Statistical Manual of Mental Disorders (American Psychiatric Association, 2013), an experience of trauma is described as follows:

- An exposure to threat.
- A presence of symptoms related to a post-trauma event.
- A persistent avoidance of stimuli associated with a trauma event.
- A negative alteration in cognition and mood, associated with a traumatic event.
- A marked alteration in arousal and reactivity, associated with a traumatic event.

- A long duration of disturbance.
- A disturbance that causes significant distress.

While diagnostic labels do predict certain patterns of behaviour, they can tautologically confer problems, causality, and disempowerment for children (Strong, 1995). With unaccompanied asylum-seeking children, it is critical that we understand the ethical postures we take and the need for collaborative practice.

We have been inspired in part by Post-Structuralism (Foucault, 2003) and Tomm (1990, 1998) to be mindful about using the term *refugee* as a political act. It can support the dominance of politicians and professionals. It can also support the submissiveness of the person so named 'refugee' or an 'asylum-seeking' individual (Tomm, 1998; Schwartz, 1999). Tomm (1990) has critiqued this type of diagnostic labelling, asserting that all interactions with those we work with are potential interventions. They require us to consider the ethical implications of our interactions. He also asserts that, in the work we do, we are not only engaged in matters of heuristics but also of ethics and politics. This is how we need to make sense of how we go on together (Tomm, 1987a, 1987b, 1988).

When we bring together the *Location, Dislocation, and Relocation* practice framework with the Medical Approach (later shown in Table 1) in the understanding of trauma, it is helpful to think about when we would use the different possibilities each brings. We also pay attention to the meaning created for the person who is being described.

'Hussain's Human Rights Assessment was coming shortly. The prospect of him becoming Appeal Rights Exhausted was very real, hence his heightened anxieties. At very short notice, Ana offered to see him at an office in London. After an hour, Ana brought out an ashen Hussain. He went off to the WC. In those brief moments, Ana told me of hypervigilance, flashbacks, dark, suicidal thoughts, self-harm, and other symptoms, all of which were linked to what could be described as a post-traumatic stress response. Ana prepared a detailed report for his human rights assessment. There was also a report from the Refugee Council concerning the support she had given. Another report from the Red Cross Family Tracing Service said that they had searched exhaustively and unsuccessfully for his mother and three sisters and that his case was now closed. The final evidence was a copy of the photo of historical self-harm.'

(Izzy, volunteer teacher and advocate)

This story describes the bringing forth of distinctions as ethical and political acts of power. It suggests that when I, (Ana co-author) chooses to use certain linguistics (rather than other descriptions that could have been employed in the same situation), I have explicitly chosen a particular political position in relation to the phenomenon being described (Tomm, 1992).

It is a description of how the Medical Approach and its situated explanation were the most useful in meeting Hussain's needs. From the accounts given, others were able to make sense of the impact of *dislocation* on him. That is not to say that he had no *locating* stories or *relocating* abilities, but rather, the Medical Approach was more useful as a paradigm, given its context.

Table 1 describes the distinctions among the different ways of working.

Table 1 The *Location, Dislocation, and Relocation* practice framework and the Medical Approach

The Location, Dislocation, and Relocation *framework*	*Medical Approach*
Situated meaning: meaning dependent on context	*Grand narrative*: applied to a context to make sense of what seems senseless through its own lens
Idiolect: language as distinct to an individual	*Master code*: an assumption of universality in language
The difference that makes a difference: orientation to the present and solutions	*Original cause*: fixation on the past, understanding the original cause, and creating a trajectory of cause-effect
Inter-determinacy: understanding the complex and nuanced ways we influence and are influenced by those we work with	*Determinacy*: fixed structures and narratives that are separate from the practitioner, observer, and professional
Becoming: evolving through life story (past, present, and future)	*Being*: fixed by past descriptors

The *Location, Dislocation, and Relocation* practice framework takes a 'both/and' position. This is where various things can be simultaneously true and where every individual experience has its own reality, despite what another individual might experience. The context in which we act guides the meaning of the language we use and the identity that best fits the story we, and others, have of ourselves.

'In a teaching session with two secondary schools, I demonstrated the different conversations I had, according to context. For example, talking to my young son by saying something like, "Bunny rabbit, I can't wait to see you later today." I then talked about how inappropriate it would be to use this familiarity with the headmaster, whom I had only met a couple of times. The headmaster quipped that he would quite like to be called "bunny rabbit," to much hilarity from those attending.'

(Ana, co-author)

As reported in Table 1, a grand narrative is an institutional and ideological form of knowledge from which meaning is shaped and understanding is created (Lyotard, 1979). The medicalised approach of trauma can be seen as positioning people into a narrative that lacks a situated meaning. This can create a way of thinking that is a 'grand' narrative. It is where the person who experiences trauma is identified and seen only through this lens. The linguistics associated with a grand narrative are, for instance, 'You are traumatised,' which can shape the identity of the individual hosting the trauma. The person's presenting problem can become the problem and, in turn, the focus from which an enquiry is made. Often, young people are only aware of this narrative. It then becomes a single story of who they are and what they can be. It does not look at other stories that are based on aspects of *location*, such as familial resources, abilities, and connections. They are so much more than the trauma narrative we give them – they are a son, a brother, a cricketer, a footballer, and a friend.

> 'Abel looked at me, embarrassed. He asked if he could tell me something that he hadn't told anyone else. I reassured him that he didn't have to tell me anything. It was OK for me not to know. He insisted that he wanted me to know and understand more about his experiences while at the Jungle in Calais. He went on to tell the story of going with friends to the parked lorries, trying to find a 'lift' to the UK. He described the laughter they would have and their comradery in being together as they sought passage. "It wasn't all bad," he told me. "Those moments with friends were really good."'
>
> (Ana, co-author)

A grand narrative is enforced by a 'master code' or diagnosis (e.g. Post-Traumatic Stress Disorder or Obsessive-Compulsive Disorder). This is where a list of characteristics forms the code that categorises and understands a lived experience. Although this 'master code' might not reflect a meta narrative or contextual meaning, it can be a fixed way of describing one's story. What we have often seen is that services require the 'master code' before offering support to the young person.

From a hierarchical perspective, a medical trauma approach starts from a place of *dislocation*. It starts from an assumed position and fixes the meaning given within the grand narrative, where you are either traumatised or not. It also talks about 'original cause,' including any abuse and maltreatment that has been experienced. Often, the system speaks about these young people by starting with their *dislocated* stories. This defines the young person's story among professionals. The system's language becomes a *dislocated* language in which the young person's story is told.

Abel, in his story, demonstrates this in his need to tell a different story about himself. It does not mean that adverse experiences didn't take place, but rather that they did. Furthermore, other relational experiences that were a form of community and togetherness in the dilemmas they all faced also emerged.

As per Table 1, the danger of only having a Medical Approach is that it could be led by the principle of original cause and the determinacy of who someone is and what they can do. The original experience, or experiences, are defined as traumatising. The individual is then perceived to inhabit and 'be' the trauma. From here, they experience certain things and behave in certain ways that are associated with this 'master code' (Draper & Marcellino, 2023a). The original cause also shapes the description as to what type of trauma the individual hosts. For example, Post-Traumatic Stress Disorder describes one traumatic event rather than a series of multiple traumatic events that are associated with complex trauma. The Medical Approach can be useful. However, this way of working can also blind us to alternative stories. During a supervision session, a supervisee brought a case to me (Elisa, co-author), describing it as follows:

'The client hoards garden tools as if they have an obsessive-compulsive disorder. This behaviour has started since they lost their father.'

Table 2 highlights the following conversation and shows a different narrative from what has been understood by the supervisee.

Table 2 Relocating in supervision

Person speaking	What was said
Elisa:	'What did the client like doing with their father?'
Jenny:	'They liked gardening together.'
Elisa:	'What does it mean for them to garden today?'
Jenny:	'To continue doing what he enjoyed with his father.'
Elisa:	'They are buying garden tools because they enjoyed gardening with their father, and they would like to still enjoy these activities.'
Jenny:	'Yes, perhaps it keeps them connected to their father.'
Elisa:	'So, the client is reconnecting with their father through the things they liked doing together. He is collecting memories.'

Location, Dislocation, and Relocation is a practice framework where meanings can emerge and flow. It is a narrative and social constructionist approach that considers the presenting problem/concern as, more often than not, based on a dominant story (Draper & Marcellino, 2023b). This is challenged in therapeutic work by evaluating the alternatives that are often hidden and not told (Merscham, 2000).

Just like Abel, a person who has experienced trauma does not become trauma. They will have multiple ways of experiencing and expressing their sense of self. Our work has focused on enquiring about multiple identities. This also can be understood as inter-determination and encompasses the following: gender, age, culture, race, education, religion, etc. It also links to the idea that stories are 'mutant;' they are evolving and not fixed. In the flow of communication, we are developing the stories that are lived and told. Tomm (1991) describes these as patterns of interaction that significantly influence each other's experience. He describes how we move from linear assumptions to circular ones. These are where consequences are linked to a behaviour, which maintains the presenting problem. This way of working reframes the behaviour of concern from 'within' to 'between' people.

From a narrative perspective, the lives we lead and the relationships we hold are shaped by both the stories we develop and the meaning we give to our experiences (White & Denborough, 1998). This suggests that our life experiences are mapped into the stories that we are born into. We remember some of them, whereas we leave others untold (Freedman & Combs, 1996; Pearce & Pearce, 1990). Young people with traumatic experiences tend to internalise these adverse situations as inner conversations. These restrict the perception and description of self. They also create narratives that portray themselves and others as lacking worth or power (Adams-Westcott et al., 1993; Etchison & Kleist, 2000).

What meaning are we co-creating, and what kind of stories do these meanings translate into? This is what Tomm (1991) would describe as 'wholeness interpersonal patterns' rather than 'pathologizing interpersonal patterns.' The danger of 'pathologizing' and 'individualising' is that the system around the individual interprets communication as a fixed story with no possibility to thrive (Tomm et al., 2014).

Location, Dislocation, and Relocation

The framework starts with the self and identity because, in the humanising and normalising of the other, we can start to understand where connections can be made. The 'I,' which is 'me,' is the person who looks with a certain focus and vision. They then weave together emergent patterns, from which stories are born. This links to Coordinated Management of Meaning, as we are constructing a normalisation to take place in the flow of discoveries made in the interactions we are having. We then invite the reader to join us on this journey, sharing their own experiences and viewpoints as we travel together. In doing this, we want to start from our own selves, to develop together a source of knowledge in which we are able to interchange from the 'I' to the 'we.' A key principle in this way of working is that we are not fixing the trauma. We are trying to make sense of the trauma through listening and curiosity.

> 'Shila was from Iran and was the manager of the reception centre where unaccompanied children were placed on arrival in the UK. She talked about being a tomboy as a child. She loved climbing trees, something she had not done since coming to the UK ten years previously. She was motherlike to some of the young people and would encourage them to walk with her. She would tell them about her tree-climbing exploits, and they would tell her about theirs. On one of the walks, a young person started to climb a tree and teased that she had forgotten how to climb. Before I knew it, she was climbing the tree, and some of the other children were also joining in. Shila's story had been listened to and interpreted as an invitation to play and, through that play, to connect together.'
>
> (Ana, co-author)

In that moment, Shila co-created a tree-climbing story in which all the previous tree-climbing episodes were present and would become a new future story. That said, the local authority was not best pleased from a health and safety perspective!

We have seen a rise in professionals' use of 'safe places,' with the premise that safety is something known and an experience that can be accessed. In the *Location, Dislocation, and Relocation* framework, we do not use the linguistics of 'safe' as it can function as a single descriptor. Instead, we use the geographical language of *location*, with the multiplicity of possibilities it supports. Language moves us, so it is important to be careful of the language we use, with assumptions about what it will mean.

When we think about 'safety,' there is no such thing in some children's world. Thinking about what has previously been described and assumed to be safe can remind them of how out of control their childhoods have been. Their more intimate places – their home, room, bed, and often body – were in that place of 'safety,' which was repeatedly violated.

Cronen & Lang (1994) spoke about 'meaning as use.' This refers to knowing the meaning of a word or a sentence, which is linked to knowing how to use it within the specific context in which it is uttered. In the use of language in our work, we often find that the word *safety* leads the young person to an unwanted and difficult place.

Some years ago, a friend wrote about a 'field' as a humanly created open space that facilitates a sense of cultural memory. He contended that a field is neither good nor bad; it is neutral. It is a place we can inhabit, a place that facilitates a type of haunting. This type of haunting is not supernatural but totally human. It requires a place to occur, that place being a field, and the human a receptacle to admit our ghost (Davis, 2005). These ideas are linked to Derrida's (1994) claim that the linguistic use of haunting is a way of describing and defining a sense of justice. Derrida spoke about the past repeating and returning in the present, demanding acknowledgment for an unheard message in the past. Fisher (2012), just like Derrida, also spoke about hauntology as an element of time. It is divided into two temporal aspects: no longer and not yet. In both instances, there is either a sense of repetition or anticipation.

'"I can't go to a safe place," Afri told us.'

When we explored the idea of a safe place and what that might mean to her, she explained that when she is in such a place, it means that danger is heightened. Going there puts her at risk. Things become unearthed, and danger is more present. The space is a battlefield, with remnants of the past littering the present.

As we explored this further together, she was able to explain that vigilance is a friend because it helps her to know when to run or hide. If she were to stop and relax, anything could happen. In trying to reach refuge, I (Ana, co-author) returned to the idea of a safe space with Afri. We entered a circular conversation with punctuation and transitions with distant memories, moments lived, and harms averted. I (Ana, co-author) returned to ask questions about the need to maintain vigilance and who could do this for her so that she could get the justice she deserves.

'"I'm not sure I'm ready to go there yet," she told me.'

We held the word *yet*. It is a big word with potential and possibility. It is a bridging word towards a *location* where she has memory and the possibility of a different type of haunting – the present haunted from the future, one that acknowledges the past and, from this, grows a new topsoil that shapes life. In being in the field as a *location*, I (Ana, co-author) notice that a field is different from a city, where the landscape is concrete and a footprint can't be made. In Afri's field, she has the footprints of her foster parents, their parents, and her community. She is not alone. There are others there, and the footprint serves as a way of guarding against and connecting with long-gone footprints that are kicked, trampled, and bled.

We came to realise how justice was slowly coming together. Therefore, her life is not described as a curriculum vitae but as a series of possibilities, connections, and new experiences. These shape a basic cycle: the day, the week, the month, and the season. The possibility of what we are producing, together with her foster family, is part of informally told narrative histories. These act as a basic activity from which meaning is made of her actions. It is a feature of all communal memory. It is the fabric from which new stories are made and a life is grown (Connerton, 1989).

Location is understood as a sense of place. It can be used to simply describe where a place is on a map. However, the meaning is more complex. Each place has a different meaning to different people and is therefore highly personal, experiential, and subjective. A particular market square, building, or café is likely to mean different things to different people depending on what has happened to them (or others) there. The same place can be a *located* story for some and a *dislocated* story for others, depending on what has happened to them (or others) there. The same place can be a *located* story for some and a *dislocated* story for others.

In the following paragraphs, we describe three different stories from a *location* perspective. We discovered, through our work together, that our stories linked to each other. The *located* stories support our own understanding of what *location* is. They also link us together in our knowledge of *located* stories for each other. We had not made connections to our own sense of *location* as migratory, but this helped to shape our interactions and those of the people we work with.

'I enjoy going to an Italian café with some of my friends. It is a place that reminds me of my home country, where I can speak Italian and eat Italian food. This includes an embodied experience through sight, smell, sound, and taste. The same place would not have the same meaning to everyone who visits it.'

(Elisa, co-author)

'The smell of the seaside reminds me of my birthplace, Jersey. One of the earliest memories I have is walking along the beach with a family friend and their dog. A positive embodied experience through the smell and the sights.'

(Samantha, co-author)

'"Give me plantains and eggs! That," as my dad used to say, "is the food of the heavens." He should know; he was a missionary after all! The smell of plantains and eggs is still one of my favourite things. When I was waiting for a tumour to be removed from my head, my dad cooked me plantains and eggs. It was the meal we shared before the pre-surgery fast.'

(Ana, co-author)

A sense of place then refers to the meanings associated with that place. The meaning is the way we *locate* our sense of self in a place. For Elisa, it is an Italian cafe; for Samantha, it is the beach and seaside; and for Ana, it is plantains and eggs.

As per Shila's story, she was able to bring previous *locations* of tree climbing into the present. Therefore, she was able to show that the way we have been *located* in the past is the way in which we can bring that experience, as a resource, to life in the present. In knowing ourselves as *located* and helping others to also discover their *located* stories, we are supporting them to find a way of creating a space in which they have mastery. This can be identified in protocols from a clinically approved, evidence-based trauma protocol called Eye Movement Desensitisation and Reprocessing (EMDR Institute, 2022). Eye Movement Desensitisation and Reprocessing has a focus on expanding a 'safe place' from which an enhancement of this experience can occur. Schools and those caring for children who have experienced trauma have also been encouraged to support children in finding a physical place where they feel contained. This means that when they are *dislocated*, they have somewhere to go. Yet, *location* is much more than just safety. It is the revisiting of a world that is made up of a sense of being and belonging, of connecting and being connected.

Location is embodied. It is perceptual, cognitive, linguistic, and soulful. The following are descriptors of each of these:

• Embodied – where we feel different sensations in our body and head.
• Perceptual – what is made of that story by others.
• Cognitive – the effects on the neuro-brain of those thinking patterns.
• Linguistic – oral communication of the experiences and stories we have.
• Soulful – the sense of others in the sacred and spiritual.

Location is a map from which we define the story we tell and how we tell it. This type of *location* indicates an entity with an ambiguous boundary. It relies more on the human or social attributes of identity and sense of place.

'It was a cold, rainy October when I moved to England. I was wearing a long coat while pushing two suitcases that contained everything important to me. A picture of my parents when I was a child, a small flag of my home country, and food – of course there was food! My family managed to pack cheese, bread, and salami in my suitcases to the point where I struggled to close them. When I arrived at my new room in London, I was embraced by the colours inside the luggage. I cried.'

(Elisa, co-author)

The framework supports how we can *locate* many aspects of the life a person has lived. We can use the stories that shape identity as human beings and span a person's horizons. As professionals, we understand that an individual's experiences create a vision bias. This is a tool that can be used to shape curiosity when with another person. Often, *location* stories are unknown or untold. This is because the focus of the system around the individual only asks questions from a place of *dislocation*. We therefore 'fix' a person into stories of 'being' *dislocated* rather than in the movement between *Location, Dislocation and* the *Relocation* that is always taking place.

Dislocation encompasses the processes and characteristics within periods of geographical *dislocation* – in particular, the move away from the familiar to the unfamiliar and from the known to the unknown (Draper & Marcellino, 2023a). Those who have experienced agency and mastery, along with those young people who have become more silent and less proficient, both experience *dislocation*.

> '"I'm safe, but how can I be happy? My loved ones are sick or in danger of dying." I remember with sadness the day when Abram told me that one of his friends had, on hearing sad news from home, taken his own life and died alone in a London bedsit.'
>
> (Izzy, volunteer teacher and advocate)

The physical *dislocation* of an individual involving the loss of familiar support systems (i.e. geographical *dislocation*) constitutes a significant challenge. This raises potential threats to self-esteem, destabilising ambiguity of role, stress (in regard to uncertainty), and challenges to autonomy through a reduced sense of control (Draper & Marcellino, 2023a).

Regardless of whether the geographical *dislocation* is desired or undesired, there is often confusion and preoccupation with the characteristics of the new environment and the loss of the old one (Draper & Marcellino, 2023a). These contextual stresses are more particularly felt when there are changes in social networks where there is a perceived loss of environmental mastery (Harris et al., 2012). This study also highlighted that those individuals who were ready and had planned their *relocation* demonstrated readiness for the challenge through purposeful and selective mastery of the new environment (Harris et al., 2012).

Here we share two of our *dislocated* stories as moments in which we link our own experience to the framework.

> 'When I moved to Scotland, I noticed that, although people looked the same, there was something unfamiliar about them. I started working with families and became aware their speech was different, with new sounds and dialects. This sometimes resulted in me being unable to understand their stories. It created a sense of being deskilled as a therapist whose work is steeped in stories and relational connections. This move created many experiences of dislocation.'
>
> (Samantha, co-author)

Linear stories start from a place of *dislocation*. Their focus is on thin stories about the present *dislocation* rather than on the ebb and flow from which their *dislocation* is being experienced (White & Epston, 1990; White, 1995). Yet, only by taking the time to become orientated to the *located* sense of self can coherence be created of the *dislocation* taking place.

'Anil was struggling to sleep and had started to wander out of his shared house onto the streets. He complained that he just couldn't rest. Lots of sleep hygiene (Chapter 5) work was done. He had a sleep pack. We tried to help him reverse his body clock, but he still could not sleep. Only when I asked him about where he had been when he was last able to sleep and who was there with him did his lack of sleep start to make sense. He was sleeping in a room by himself in a shared house in the middle of a busy city that was never fully dark. Whereas, before leaving Afghanistan, he had lived in a small village and slept on the floor of his family hut. He had slept with all his family on the same floor, and he could hear their breathing and feel their movements near him. He could also smell and feel the animals that slept on the same floor. His hut was completely dark, with only the night sky to break the darkness. When we started to understand the dislocation he was experiencing, we realised that to enable him to sleep, we needed to support him to relocate. He needed to be in an environment that replicated the characteristics of when sleep had been present. His social worker was able to move him to a foster family who lived on a farm. Anil found the ability to sleep with a collie dog on a hard mattress bed and a night sky, with only the stars breaking the darkness.'

(Ana, co-author)

Relocation is an active action of intent. It is to move. It is the process of leaving one habitus and settling into another. Therefore, it has *dislocation* as a punctuation in the transition being made (Draper & Marcellino, 2023a). It is a move that includes packing up our stories of belongings and transferring those stories to the new home. All this while negotiating similarities and differences in the new terrain (Draper & Marcellino, 2023a).

To support *relocation*, we need to participate in rewriting the *location* story with the clients. Yet the way we listen to that story and our intent affects the 'enquiry' we make.

'Ordo was weeping at the loss of his friend. His friend had been moved to Ipswich as part of a National Transfer Scheme. Ordo had started a hunger strike to demand that he be moved to be with his friend. He was told of the plan to move to Devon, where he could start to build a life for himself here in the UK. Ordo was distraught, and his hunger strike continued. I became curious about Ordo and his friend. What was their relationship? When asked, Ordo talked about his friend being from the same village. They had both promised their families to stay together and take care of each other. On the journey they travelled together, they did take care of each other and became like brothers. We explored the migrant idea of kinship, and I began to realise that Ordo was being separated from his brother. It was only when we contacted the local authority about the kinship between Ordo and his friend that it was decided they should not be separated. The local authority gracefully extended the placement for Ordo.'

(Ana, co-author)

Location, Dislocation, and Relocation shift according to the situated meaning shaped by the characteristics of Social GGRRAAACCEEESSS (Burnham, 2012; see Figure 2.1).

These social characteristics are defined as: gender, geography, race, religion, ability/disability, age, appearance, culture, class, education, employment, ethnicity, sexuality, sexual orientation, and spirituality. The differing characteristics are components of the context in which actions occur. Added to this, there are the *Location, Dislocation, and Relocation* episodes that also act as part of the contextual forces. From here, communication and meaning-making take place (Jensen & Penman, 2018).

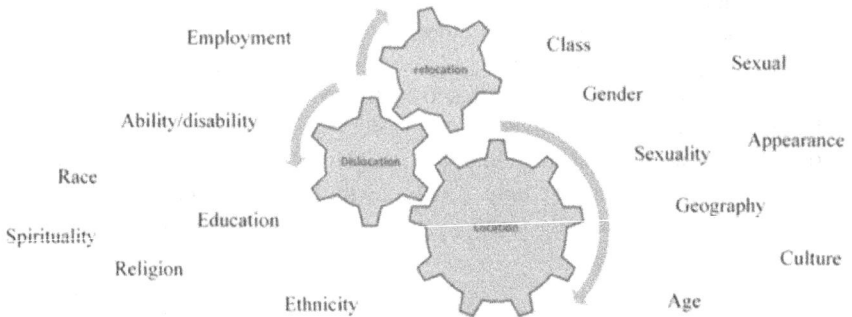

Figure 2.1 The Location, Dislocation, and Relocation in the movement, which is made from aspects of social difference.

'When I was called, I was questioned first by the Home Office official and then by the judge. "Why do you think that this particular boy is deserving of asylum?" So I recounted a story. Assem had been brought up on a farm, high up in the mountains. The farm overlooked the valley below, where the Taliban had a camp. All day long, their militia practised drills and the use of weaponry. Throughout his childhood, he listened to a continuous soundtrack of violence. One summer evening, Assem told me that, on returning to his new home from college, he had made himself a cup of tea. He told me that he sat outside in the garden, surrounded by the rubbish and cans left by previous tenants. As he sipped his tea, he listened to his neighbours chatting, laughing, and cooking supper while children were playing and teenagers were playing music – everyday domestic murmurings. Assem told me, without embarrassment, "Teacher, my face was suddenly wet with tears, but I wasn't sad. I realised this is the sound of PEACE." As I recounted Assem's account to the judge, I looked up and saw her wiping a tear from her eye. Later, in her summing up, she quoted back at me my final words to her: "All this boy wants is peace and a safe haven."'

(Izzy, volunteer teacher and advocate)

The framework at work

The emergent new understanding of the use of this framework has helped us, as co-authors, co-create the *relocating tools*. These are the *Distress Screening Tool* (described in Chapter 4), *Sleep Work* (in Chapter 5), *Nutrition Work* (in Chapter 6), the *Continuing Bonds Enquiry* (in Chapter 7), and *Fast Feet Forward* (in Chapter 8).

'In my work with hosting families who offered their homes to Ukrainian refugees, it was important that information about how the host family worked, including times for breakfast and dinner, were kept in the kitchen. Other information, such as details of local transport, was contained in an information booklet. This supported the guests to relocate upon their arrival.'

(Samantha, co-author)

To enable this narrative *location* to happen, we need to engage in curious questions that support a mutation of new possibilities.

Examples of *location* questions a young person should be guided to ask themselves are as follows:

- Who am I in that place?
- What sensory experiences am I having when *located* there?
- Where does it take me in my emotions?
- Who is there with me?
- What does that place mean to me?
- How can I let others know about the meaning the place has for me?

Embodied questions could also support a thickening of the sense of *location*. Often, we do not ask embodied questions because we do not think that our body is part of the story. However, traumatic experiences are often linked to somatic symptoms. These are expressions of the body's memory as a result of the trauma (Caizzi, 2012). During times of *dislocation*, embodied experiences are present. Young people often describe this as having stomach aches, feeling sick, and, in the main, for unaccompanied children, headaches. Therefore, in *locating* questions, we need to support storytelling about the body so that coherence can be formed in the stories our bodies are telling.

The types of questions we could use are:

- Am I up or down?
- How high or how low am I?
- How dark or light is it? (Some young people like darkness to hide, and some like light to be alert.)
- What is my skin telling me about the atmosphere?
- Where is my breath?
- What are the sensations in my stomach?

These questions enhance a sense of understanding of our embodied experience and help to know a young person from a sense of *location*. It is important to notice what our breathing is doing and what it is telling us about the place we are in. One's stomach can be a descriptor of how we are (e.g. starving, full, digesting).

There are also soulful types of questions, such as:

- What am I grateful for?
- What kind of grace am I experiencing?
- What kindness is in this moment?
- When is gentleness present?

These types of questions proactively seek to elicit stories and descriptions from which coherence about a given *location* is shaped. Coordination takes place in the interactions of individuals' lived stories, as told by the narrator. There is a sense of mystery to the other actors' lived realities. It is in the story told about the described *locating* interaction. Therefore, *location* is not objective or measurable but rather subjective and subtle.

As therapists, we strive to retain a place of reflection from our own *Located, Dislocated, and Relocated* stories. These stories shape our listening and interactional patterns and, therefore, the responses we are likely to make. It is the way we humanise and normalise the *Location, Dislocation, and Relocation* stories we are being told. We have found that we need to be in the continued flow of the following questions as a way of enabling new understandings to become a lived possibility:

- What do we notice is common to us all?
- What is the normalising process we are doing together?
- What are the links between us?

We ask these questions because, in the movement between *Location, Dislocation, and Relocation*, we are inviting others to be active and involved in the role of *relocation*.

Draper & Hannah (2008) talked about enabling new understandings by reflecting on the implications of the conversation itself. They advocated a relational curiosity from which they explored what had been said in the conversation and what might be helpful to then collaborate and coordinate together.

In Chapter 1, we started with Alex, an adult who had the experience of being an unaccompanied minor. It is a story full of *Location, Dislocation, and Relocation*. He gives you this story as a way in which you can join his story, to hear his *location, dislocation*, and how he *relocates* himself. Think of the questions you might want to ask him using this framework. See the opportunities for enhancing *relocation* by exploring *located* stories.

To familiarise yourself with this way of working, write your own story and then use the *Location, Dislocation, and Relocation* framework against your own *locating* stories. Notice how, in moments of *dislocation*, you *relocate* yourself. Here are examples of co-author Ana doing this when she mapped some of her own story within the practice framework. For the full story, see Draper (2018).

Location:

'We lived in a place called Santo Domingo de los Colorados. This was, at that time, a small village close to the jungle and a tribal group called the Tsachila. My parents called our home 'Buckingham Palace' because it was a shack built on stilts to keep away snakes. They liked the juxtaposition of such a name. My mother tells of the British ambassador who, when passing by and seeing the sign to the house, stopped to investigate who lived there. He was delighted when she gave him a jam tart and tea. He proclaimed that she was the 'Queen of Harts,' as Hart was our family surname.'

Dislocation:

'When I was nine, my parents decided to come back to the UK. I want to make this a short and sharp sentence because that is how it felt. We arrived in winter to a very cold and icy house, where before I had been used to the abundant warmth of both the climate and the people. This was like being frozen, both from a physical and an identity perspective. I had no English, no cultural connections, and everything that I was screamed difference. I heard my grandmother whisper to my dad, "John, they are natives," as she tried to acclimatise to these strangers who were somehow connected to her. I was in vertigo; nothing made sense. I did not belong, and I even had to wear shoes on my feet!'

Relocation:

'At night, I would cry. I would dream that I was with my adopted sister in Ecuador and that England was some sort of nightmare that I would wake from, and then it would all go away. This was a repeat dream on a loop, recurring time and again. Sometimes, I would go and find my dad and cry in his arms as he comforted me back to sleep. I longed for familial food. So, occasionally, Dad would go to London and bring home some mangoes or plantains. The delight and feeling of homecoming this brought was a relief to the home sickness I was experiencing.'

Location, Dislocation, and Relocation **as a recursive ongoing cycle:**

'When I returned to Ecuador, the cycle and stories continued. I met with a woman who had been a significant part of my childhood, and while sitting and holding her sleeping great-grandchild on her lap, I had a wonderful memory of her doing that for me when I was a child, in the same church. It was lovely to see that, after more than 40 years, she had not lost her touch.'

As you can see from these descriptions, this framework has no ending; it is a continuous and evolving process from which meaning is thickened and new stories are told.

Outsider Witness reflection notes you may want to make about Chapter 2 are as follows:

- What in the chapter did I *locate* to?
- What in the chapter did I *dislocate* from?
- What would I want to *relocate* with in the future?

What 'sense' do I make of this narrative framework within different aspects of who I am?

- What hopes did it create?
- If the framework were made up of colour, what colour would it be?
- How much of the framework could I map my lived experience to?
- What soulful connections am I making?
- How will this change what I might, or might not, do next?
- What new interactions does this way of thinking create in collaboration with unaccompanied asylum-seeking children?

Chapter 3

A physiological perspective of trauma

When using the *Location, Dislocation, and Relocation* framework, it is important to think of *dislocation* as a way in which a young person starts to tell their story. It is also important to try to understand who they are and the agency they have in their relationships. These factors can contribute to a fixed way of seeing things, from which future choices and decisions are made.

The good news is that our brains have a remarkable ability to change. This process was first reported by William James (1890) when describing the plasticity of the nervous system. Brain plasticity, also known as neuroplasticity, involves adaptive structural and functional change (Puderbaugh & Emmady, 2022). It appears that the ability of the brain to rearrange itself is present throughout every life stage (Doidge, 2007). It is especially responsive and prominent in young brains (Murdock, 2020), forming new paths while old pathways become pruned. In this chapter, we describe how it is that often children and young people who have experienced multiple *dislocations* are not supported to be other than the person they have become in response to their experience. It is important to see that they are not fixed in their identity, and through changes that occur in their responses and in the brain, they can reclaim the person they want to be.

Brain plasticity is the ability of the brain to reinforce experience. The repetition of these types of experiences is critical in influencing the brain's ability to form new pathways through which new ways of managing distress can be accessed. It is a collaborative process from which these new experiences and behaviours are coordinated and negotiated as a repeat process from which children and young people who have experienced trauma find new ways to manage their emotions.

'Ahmed's asylum claim had been rejected by the Home Office. They felt that he was withholding information as he struggled to speak and tell his story. The stories he did tell did not connect to known events. It was felt, therefore, that his claim for asylum was not warranted. Ahmed was distraught. His ability to remember aspects of his story in the firing line of questions had become compromised. In his distress, he would lose the ability to think and remember what had happened. He was not able to voice the truth about his experiences. Ahmed had one last appeal hearing with the Home Office. He was terrified that he would

DOI: 10.4324/9781003258681-4

freeze and be unable to speak and tell his story again. In the conversation we had, I focused on location stories – who his parents had been, where they had lived, what kind of food they had eaten together, the things they would say to each other, etc. We started to build the ability for him to be present as that young person, with a family, a name, and a community. In amplifying his identity as Ahmed, who is a son, a brother, a cricketer, and a comedian, we were able to support him in amplifying his voice from a located place. On his appeal, he described being able to, in the terror of the questions being asked, hold his voice, tell his story, and, for the first time, be coherent.'

(Ana, co-author)

Distress is a by-product of *dislocation*. It is an emotional response that requires attention. The previous story connects to Walker (2013) when it speaks about the survival behaviours linked to flight and freeze.

Humans are complex. When placed in the interrelated wiring of systems that shape experience, such as taste, smell, and touch, they then go on to create patterns of behaviours associated with those systems. In Ahmed's story, his response to the terror of not being believed could be described as a freeze response. Ahmed expressed the desire to run away to escape the danger he felt he was in and, without support, would have acted in a flight response. When a young person is displaying this type of behaviour, it can be diagnosed as something other than a normal behaviour that is about creating safety. Often, we have found that young people who exhibit these types of behaviours can be seen to be neuro-diverse or bi-polar.

Mitigation of the impact is critical in moments of *dislocation*. We know that vulnerable children, such as unaccompanied asylum-seeking children and looked-after children, experience high levels of *dislocation*. This happens during the process of their development (Bean et al., 2007; Wiese & Burhorst, 2007; Anthony et al., 2022), and it is defined as Adverse Childhood Experiences (Felitti et al., 1998). They increase the risk of chronic physical health and poor mental health across the lifespan (Ridout et al., 2018; Bellis et al., 2014; Hambrick et al., 2018; Nicolson et al., 2023).

Here is a list of symptoms that children and young people had, who visited the doctor at the general practice clinic in the Kent reception centre:

- Chest infections
- Abdominal pain
- Gastritis
- Constipation
- Diarrhoea
- Nightmares
- Sleep difficulties
- Tremors and anxiety
- Lower back pain
- Impetigo
- Scabies

- Conjunctivitis
- Skeletal pain
- Urinary tract infections
- Toothache and earache
- Burns
- Self-harming
- Oral thrush
- Lack of appetite
- Type 1 diabetes
- Malaria
- Fractured bones
- Tear gas injury to the eyes
- Rubber bullet bruising to the body
- Dizziness and shortness of breath
- Barbwire damage to nerves in the hand
- Haemoptysis
- Heart block
- Tonsillitis
- Headaches

Although this list encompasses a group of children arriving at a reception centre, an individual child showed the following (as reported by the practice nurse): **Ortho-paedic problems:** old fractures, malunions, and poor healing. **Tropical disease:** malaria. **Dental Problems:** carries, previous injuries to the palate and jaw. **Vision problems:** infection requiring an optician. **Emotional/mental health problems:** aggression, anxiety, self-harm, insomnia, night terrors, panic attacks, post-trau-matic disorders. **Skin problems:** scabies.

In relation to these children's health stories, we can see that the stories they tell about their experiences, of both transitions and critical moments, are further articulated by their bodies. We need to ensure that we look at both the physical presentation and support this to be managed, as well as being mindful of the body's response as part of a survival strategy linked to the past. At times, physical issues can be misunderstood as emotional; for example, a young person who has a urinary tract infection may become confused and erratic in their behaviour.

As highlighted, *dislocation* is made up of transitions and critical moments. Some are developmentally generic for any child. Others are associated with addi-tional displacement connected to the circumstances that shape vulnerability. These Adverse Childhood Experiences include direct and indirect experiences such as abuse, parental conflict, and substance misuse within their living environment (Hughes et al., 2017).

Another identified category is intergenerational trauma, which acknowledges exposure to adverse life experiences as being passed from a trauma survivor to their descendants. This concept was first introduced by Rakoff et al. (1966) in their study about the offspring of Holocaust survivors. There is growing research about the offspring effect that follows parental experiences of trauma. These include those who were veterans, those exposed to genocide and slavery, and those who experienced childhood maltreatment (Yehuda & Bierer, 2009; O'Toole et al., 2017; Eyerman, 2001; De Gruy, 2005).

There are many ways to understand intergenerational trauma; one of these is 'our bodies keeping the score' (Van Der Kolk, 2014). This shapes our brain and its pathways, which can become attuned to survival. Using this understanding, young people who experienced intergenerational trauma can present with symptoms and patterns from traumatic events that have been experienced by previous generations. Even our DNA function, or gene transcription, changes according to our lived experience (Ridout et al., 2018; Clarke & Vieux, 2015; Bohacek & Mansuy, 2015). Therefore, the binary argument of nature versus nurture is in the process of being dispelled as we learn to understand the physiological complexity involved.

> 'Amanuel, a young person I worked with, said, "Do you know why I always end up in prison? Prison is like home." I then realised that prison was the only stable place he had ever known and the only consistency he had ever experienced.'
>
> (Elisa, co-author)

Alongside the many descriptions of what trauma is, it is important to include transitions as a *dislocating* event – for example, the number of times an unaccompanied asylum-seeking child, who is also a looked-after child, has to move placements, with the associated disruptions to friendship groups, education, etc. The adversity of the transition to a new environment and the associated changes to structure, social rules, culture, and relationships are complex. There follow multiple *dislocating* experiences that result in distress.

> 'Little Mo was brought by the police to the reception centre as a place of safety. He looked no more than 12 years old and had been placed with foster carers on arrival in the UK. Yet he had become violent toward them. He had to be removed from their home late at night and taken to a place of safety. Little Mo did not trust adults. He talked about being a man, about being 16. He described living on the streets in his home country and making money for his family to survive. His father, who was disabled and addicted to painkiller drugs, could not work. His mother was not allowed to work because of her gender. Little Mo had been told he could make more money for his family in Europe, and he had trailed older boys to arrive in the UK. Little Mo kept asking to be moved into accommodation with other peers. Another attempt to move him into foster care had failed when he had kicked, punched, and run away from his social worker. He wanted to work to send money back to his family. The only way this could happen in the UK was if he was 16. To be 12 years old was anathema to him. It was highly distressing. It meant that he couldn't care for his family.'
>
> (Samantha, co-author)

In the lived experience of *dislocations* taking place, distress is often a signal of the impact this is having on a child. Monitoring and reducing distress levels is, arguably, key to a child's ability to *relocate* to resources that enhance their well-being.

Dislocation of the brain

Neural connectors in the brain are pathways created by human experience. These are integrated into the development of the brain and its synaptic connections (Greenough et al., 1987; Greenough & Black, 1992). These authors differentiate between two forms of experiences that guide brain development: 'expectant' and 'dependent.' Experiences that are 'expected' mean that every human's brain relies on the same basic and typical experience. These allow the nervous system to develop normally. Therefore, the brain relies on essential exposure to environmental inputs. When this does not occur, the brain is affected. For instance, studies on the visual systems of animals have highlighted how the deprivation of normal vision widely impacts the performance of this system (Hubel & Wiesel, 1970; Hirsch & Spinelli, 1970; Spinelli, 1970).

Black & Greenough (1986) discussed 'experience-dependent' development as the ability of the brain to encode new experiences during its entire life. New experiences can reshape the existing structure of the brain, allowing the individual to adapt to the future of their environment. The 'experience-dependent' development means that each individual has a unique brain that depends on the idiosyncratic experiences they have had throughout their lives.

> 'Hamid rolled his eyes again. It had become a ritual between us, with me going through the solution-focused part of the Distress Screening Tool and him wanting to bypass that bit. Yet, in the 'doing,' we started to notice how much more he was able to find solutions in the moments of distress. He had found ways of telling people what he needed and helping them to help him. He was in control in a way that helped him rather than got him into trouble. "Practice makes permanent," I would say, and we would laugh together.'
>
> (Kate, clinician)

In people who have experienced repeated traumas, when using the *Location, Dislocation, and Relocation* framework, we see the traumas as *dislocations*. The brain begins to adapt to the environment and the need to keep a person safe. In an environment where there is a threat, the brain is highly functional and attuned to survival. Thus, *dislocations* have an effect on the brain's development (Bremner, 2006). *Dislocation* is what we have to become in response to repeated experiences of being unsafe and in an unknown place. For example, we might be volatile as a way to ward off any potential attack. We become unfamiliar and unknown even to ourselves in that the volatility is something that happens as part of our ability to create safety in a given moment. We should not mistake this volatility as an identity, but rather something we do in response to the dangers that are being managed and faced.

> 'When visiting London for an appointment with Esmat, I explained that both Diwali and Bonfire Night (5 November) were coming up. Each celebration required fireworks. We left the train and were walking back to my car. A firework banger exploded nearby, and something was triggered in Esmat's mind. He covered his head with his hands, screaming. He then ran in a zigzag manner, stopping under a stone archway, where he rolled himself into a ball, shaking. I crouched beside him and said, "It's only a firework – Tashwish Nakho," which means 'Don't worry' in his own language. Esmat later told me he'd been in an air raid in Afghanistan; he and his mother and younger siblings had to run for cover.'
>
> (Izzy, volunteer teacher and advocate)

Esmat's brain had assumed someone was firing at him, and he ran in a zigzag to avoid being shot. He learned to do this in the context of him and others being shot at. It is a way to protect himself from the imminent danger his brain alerts him to. The parts of the brain involved in the neural circuitry of stress include the amygdala, the prefrontal cortex, and the hippocampus (Bick & Nelson, 2016; McLaughlin et al., 2014; Teicher & Samson, 2016).

Numerous studies demonstrate that Adverse Childhood Experiences (Felitti et al., 1998; Nicolson et al., 2023) can negatively impact the structure and function of the amygdala, the subcortical area of our brain. It is the area involved in the emotional processing of information as well as socio-emotional development (De Bellis & Zisk, 2014; Hackman et al., 2010; Oshri et al., 2019). There are volumetric changes associated with the impact of Adverse Childhood Experiences on the amygdala. These can have long-term consequences, such as diminished regulation and reward processing (Haas & Canli, 2008; Harrison & Critchley, 2007; Goodkind et al., 2015). Consequences can further include the emergence of affective psychopathology, such as anxiety and depression (Gatt et al., 2009; Hanson et al., 2015). Young people who have experienced multiple adverse life events are more likely to develop an attentional bias toward fearful stimuli. This, in turn, can lead to difficulties in emotion regulation.

Critical moments are life events that impact the sense of well-being a young person experiences. An unaccompanied asylum-seeking child may have a critical moment when they hear of further turbulence in the place they have had to run from. This place may still host their family. Critical moments are beyond transitions, although linked to them. A critical moment may create further transition, and vice versa.

The following story is not an extraordinary experience for some of these children. Yet for us, it is not one we share easily, as we find the memory of this young person's distress palpable but do not want to silence his experience. We think about the impact on us of sharing this as an echo of that car bomb exploding.

> 'The news at that time was bad for some of the young people. A car bomb had been deliberately detonated in a Turkish bazaar frequented by refugees passing

through their country. The dead and wounded ran into hundreds. Fahad arrived at the reception centre that day and was immediately called aside by a social worker. He had lost 28 members of his immediate family in that bomb blast. The social worker had Fahad on suicide watch for the next 24 hours as his distress was so consuming and overwhelming.'

(Andy, mental health nurse)

The literature shows how threats, including witnessing domestic abuse, are associated with reduced hippocampus, amygdala, and ventromedial prefrontal cortical volumes (Bick & Nelson, 2016; McLaughlin et al., 2014). What we have noticed in our work with unaccompanied minors is that they struggle to recall events. They have difficulty emotionally regulating themselves. Also, their ability to manage everyday tasks, such as planning and decision-making, is impaired. They become the person who can't remember, the person who is out of control, and in our response, we need to support them to think about who they can be beyond those descriptions.

This has been a useful way to understand and make sense of different behavioural presentations in response to one's environment. Similar to when we have been on a boat and we come onto dry land, our body continues to move with the motion of the water. It is only as we become acclimated to our new environment and experience dry land that our physiological system adapts. In time, our bodies adapt, and we move away from movements and behaviours that are learned in response to the motion of the water. Yet, we need to be in a different context, with different environmental experiences that reattune our system.

'Abul explained what had happened. He had been in a bar with friends when two boys approached him. He thought they were being friendly and started to talk to them. One of the boys started to shout at him to go 'home,' and the other was punching the air and calling him racist names. "Before I knew it, I took a glass from the bar counter, smashed it, and used it to punch the boy who was shouting. There was blood everywhere, and I realised that his face was bleeding from the glass I had used. I couldn't believe I had done this; it was so automatic. It felt like I was about to be tortured again. I just let fly."'

(Elisa, co-author)

Abul responds to the racist taunt by fighting to protect himself. This was often his response to the experience of threat as an automatic way to stop himself from being attacked. When someone has this type of response, the behaviour can mimic what is described as an antisocial personality disorder. There is a danger that the person's identity becomes who they are perceived to be, rather than their behaviour being viewed as an understandable response in the context of their lived experience.

'I used to get so angry and so anxious that I wasn't safe. I used to find myself overbreathing, frozen in a lather of sweat. I used to pretend that I was okay. All I wanted was to scream and punch the walls, or even punch you. I used to take my mind somewhere else, so I felt away from others' reach. I'm learning to remain in the present, to notice my breath, and to say when I am scared, anxious, or overwhelmed. I'm learning to stay in the moment and accept it if it is uncomfortable.'

(Rabby, an unaccompanied asylum-seeking child)

In Rabby's account, we are drawn to understand his story through the lenses of the Fawn Response. The Fawn Response is a relational approach in which one person tries to appeal to and appease the threat by pleasing, calming, or minimising it to enable a sense of safety to be achieved. This can be an automatic response in which he is avoiding the threat and almost dissociating from it. He is unable to express his distress. Fawn Responses can be associated with people-pleasing behaviour, which then avoids conflicts and creates a feeling of safety. Often, we have found that young people who exhibit these types of behaviour can be diagnosed as having a personality disorder or anxiety.

Collaboration is critical in enabling a child to experience a relational and reciprocal experience in which they have agency. Much of the *dislocation* that will have taken place will have been 'done' to them. This leads to the survival activation of their brain. To enable the child to discover and experience themselves beyond what they already know, we need to support them in developing the relational skills that assist them in managing emotions and building relational connections.

'I call her because I don't know who to call. She is like a mother to me; she knows that what is happening is beyond what I can cope with. I tell her my dreams. I tell her how much I want to learn and succeed. I tell her that I am displaced, that I have no country and no place to belong. She comes with me to the embassy to state my claim for citizenship. She believes me; she knows that I am telling the truth.'

(Lufti is talking about a volunteer who supports him.)

Yet, within the care system, we rarely put systemic ways of working into practice. These involve collaborating with children to re-experience their ability to manage their emotions on a regular basis. To enable new pathways to be formed, this regularity is key and critical as an active process from which the plasticity of the brain can be activated. We know that when a child is experiencing a transition or there is a critical moment taking place, emotion is something they will experience. In those moments, we have an opportunity to support a child in practising a different way of managing the distress they are experiencing. They can also manage the emotion through collaborative partnerships that give them the opportunity to ask for help and have their needs met. This takes time, and in the repetition of experience, a child can progressively build trust in their own response. They can also build a sense of community in which emotions can be tolerated and supported.

We need to invest with the young person in repeated acts of resistance to being defined by the multiple *dislocations* they have experienced. Together, we help them find solutions; we resist with them the idea that they are stuck with being who they have become. We are part of the relational resistance from which the confusion about who they are is reduced, and there is hope in who they can be.

Outsider Witness reflection notes you may want to make about Chapter 3 are as follows:

- Have I noticed whether and how my body has responded to what I have just read?
- What 'sense' do I make of the stories with the following aspects of who I am?
- What happens to my breath in critical moments?
- How does my stomach speak, and what does it say at different times?
- What movements does my body want to make?
- How will this change what I might, or might not, do next?
- How would this shape my relationship with the young people I work with?
- How will I notice their breath, the sounds, and the poetry that connects them?
- How will I notice the movements their body might want to make?

Chapter 4

The distress screening tool

'Lidan wept. He would weep, scream, and bang his head. He had started to pray loudly throughout the night. Chanting, then weeping, then screaming again. This had been happening in his placement for two weeks, ever since his arrival. There was no calming him, and there was no obvious trigger for his distress. Yet, it was constant and palpable – and getting worse.'

(Nat, support worker)

A transdiagnostic response to transitions and critical moments

Dalgleish et al. (2020) describe a transdiagnostic response in the following way:

'Removing the distinctions between proposed psychiatric taxa at the level of classification opens up new ways of classifying mental health problems, suggests alternative conceptualizations of the processes implicated in mental health, and provides a platform for novel ways of thinking about onset, maintenance, and clinical treatment and recovery from experiences of disabling mental distress.'

Our experience in Kent, and how we understood the behaviours and distress levels shown by children, challenged us to rethink how we classified what we were witnessing. We noticed the stigma associated with mental illness was further traumatising to these children due to the cultural taboo associated with such a description. That is why they would talk about their heads hurting as a culturally bound explanation of somatic symptoms (Krause, 1989).

This is mirrored in the 2018 Children's Society report on the mental health needs of unaccompanied asylum-seeking children. This report describes the distress signals that are communicated by unaccompanied asylum-seeking children. It further describes the lack of tools that are fit for purpose in supporting the management of previous and ongoing trauma. Generic tools are not fit for purpose, as they are only sensitive to the general population. They do not identify the brain changes that have taken place and, therefore, the different settings in which a *dislocated* child will experience emotion (Children's Society, 2018). The Children's Society also

DOI: 10.4324/9781003258681-5

describe critical moments, such as visiting the Home Office, as having a detrimental effect on a child's well-being.

In the work that took place in Kent with this group of children, the same issues were described. Children's ability to cope became compromised due to their interactions with the Home Office. They struggled during times of transition by being moved across the UK as part of a settlement process called the National Dispersal Scheme. In interactions with these children, it soon became apparent that there was a need to work alongside them. This way, we could monitor their distress levels and help them manage the anxiety they were naturally experiencing.

There was also a need to ensure that the new local authority understood a child's emotional distress. This would allow them to put measures in place to support the child's emotional health and well-being upon arrival. When a child's emotional needs are not supported, vulnerability is heightened (Copeland et al., 2007). This causes emotional dysregulation to increase the occurrence of self-harming behaviours. A study in Sweden found that unaccompanied asylum-seeking children were eight times more likely to commit suicide than the general population (Mittendorfer-Rutz et al., 2019). The British government defines children who have been in foster care as having a heightened risk of self-harm. There is a 4% higher chance of attempting suicide than in the general population (Youth Government, 2022).

In *dislocating* moments, the need to protect oneself, as previously described in Chapter 3, can mean using defensive strategies. These strategies, such as the fight, flight, freeze, and fawn responses, are adopted to survive. However, they can also come across as aggression, hostility, withdrawal, or rejecting and manipulative behaviour. All these mechanisms require control to be reclaimed so that safety is maintained. They are all an attempt to survive and protect, even when the threat is no longer a signal of danger. Yet, the brain and body can be triggered into an instinctual survival mechanism that has previously worked, although this interferes with developing helpful relational patterns, as described in Chapter 2.

'The young people and I were making a wish list of requirements for housing. For example, to live near a park or close to college, etc. Timur was always very vocal, but Suman lifted his hand and said, "I know this; I want somewhere safe." The lesson was abandoned, and I told the boys, "You call me teacher, but I know nothing. Today, you have been my teacher." For me, it was a real eye-opener into the world of these young people. At the time, and to this day, politicians tell us that refugees are here for 'economic betterment,' when, all too often, all they want is a place of safety.'

(Izzy, volunteer teacher and advocate)

We need to start mitigating the heightened risk and self-harm vulnerability that are shaped by *dislocating* experiences. Currently, unaccompanied asylum-seeking children and looked-after children only receive support when they are displaying emotional dysregulation. There is no preventative strategy that supports a child's brain to create new pathways through collaborative experiences, which can then be repeated at times of transition and critical moments. Such times are also when an emotional response is highly likely to occur. We further need to know when a child requires additional support in the management of their emotions. By the time a referral is made to children's mental health services, many opportunities will have been missed. These missed opportunities could have helped a child learn how to manage their emotions.

'When Saad arrived at the reception centre, I was asked to go and see him, as he kept telling staff he had a headache and needed help. Staff had gotten to know the coding of "I have a headache" as a way of signalling emotional distress. When we met, Saad talked about the journey he had made and the fatigue, anxiety, and losses he was experiencing. Saad and I looked at the Distress Screening Tool (described in more detail later in this chapter), and he was able to utilise the items from the tool where he needed areas of support.'

(Ana, co-author)

Distress is a core concept not only for unaccompanied asylum-seeking children but for all children who are undergoing Adverse Childhood Experiences. The concept of distress is defined as extreme anxiety, sorrow, or pain associated with the loss of control over valued life experiences. These are core responses that are common to all forms of adverse experiences. Resilience is achieved by dealing with distress and restoring well-being. The spectrum of emotional and traumatic responses requires a transdiagnostic understanding (Bentovim et al., 2023; Evans & Santucci, 2021).

Cultural differences in showing distress

Social gender, geography, race, religion, age, ability/disability, appearance, class/caste, culture, education, employment, ethnicity, sexuality, spirituality, and sexual orientation, also known as Social GGRRAAACCEEESSS (Burnham, 2012), are important factors in considering how trauma and distress present in young people and unaccompanied asylum-seeking children. All social contexts shape the different types of distress that any individual is likely to experience, as well as how a particular traumatic event is perceived. The Social GGRRAAACCEEESSS (Burnham, 2012) impact on how individuals manage and what strategies they might use, given their relationship to the single or multiple traumatic events they have experienced.

'The second request was that, as Basir was deemed to be a 'flight risk,' he was required to sign in at a designated police station on a regular monthly basis. Basir's newly appointed solicitor unsuccessfully appealed this decision. Now, I found myself escorting him to a police station, which was a train journey away from his town. It was apparent that the majority of passengers, including families with young children, were travelling for the same reason. On arrival, we learned that the police station was a further walk away, along the length of a pedestrianised shopping centre. Shopkeepers and local shoppers alike literally gasped as the refugees passed by. It was the height of Brexit and UKIP, and I heard taunts, mutterings, and even boos as the column of people passed. It was racism at its worst. A humiliating and degrading situation for all who had to make that journey. The penalty for failing to sign in meant that, at any time, you could be arrested and taken to a reception centre pending deportation. So, non-compliance was never an option. Basir had to weather that monthly degradation for months.'

(Accompanying adult)

The DSM-5 (American Psychiatric Association, 2013) introduced the term *cultural concept of distress* to describe the wide set of variations in distress across cultures. In anthropology, the cultural variation of distress has been described as 'idioms of distress' (Nichter, 1981, 2010). Nichter (2010) discussed the manifestation of distress in relation to one's cultural context and meaning, as well as its social implications. He proposed that an idiom of distress assessment was a better way to offer useful insights to clinicians in the process of conducting differential diagnosis and to provide socially and culturally informed recommendations about care management (Nichter, 2010). The author suggested paying more attention to the 'Why this?' questions rather than the 'What?' questions when referring to a particular cultural way of expressing distress. The aim is to gather a better understanding of why individuals and groups embrace different means of expressing distress at specific points in time (Crandon, 1983).

'Girma kept complaining about his head hurting. It was a recurring theme when he became overwhelmed or anxious. He would hold his head and state that it always hurt and never subsided. Girma had no history of a head injury; tests had proven negative as to a physical concern. When I asked his friend about the headaches, he told me that headaches were linked to emotional pain. This was a way of him being able to express his distress without it being a madness or mental health issue, which was taboo in his country of origin.'

(Volunteer English teacher, Kent)

There is debate about whether emotion is a universal or social construct. Yet, some would see it as biologically based and heavily influenced by the environments we live in. When considering cultural differences, there is evidence to suggest that differing emotional arousal levels can exist. These are particularly prevalent in the contrast between Western and Eastern cultures (Lim, 2016).

Kinship is an area that is important to explore, given that this group of children is unaccompanied and, by the very nature of being unaccompanied, is without the familial support that other children would expect to experience. Kinship, therefore, is made with those with whom they travel, who become the people they trust to support, take care of, or protect them. Girma trusts the volunteer teacher to explain to me (Ana, co-author) the distress he was experiencing. The volunteer teacher acts as a cultural interpreter and creates meaning between us. Greene (2019) suggests that cultural brokers, within social ties, can bridge cultures, languages, and backgrounds that are particularly important to well-being. Here is an example of the benefits of kinship ties, witnessed through Girma's story, as well as his family, those he has travelled with, and those he met here in the UK.

> 'Girma is still living with his brother. He continued at college, studying plumbing to Level 1.
>
> He passed his driving test. He still plays football with his brother and other Afghan players.
>
> When the sun shines, he plays beach volleyball with friends. He enjoys camping and climbed Mount Snowdon with Afghan friends in the summer of 2018. He keeps in touch with his Kent friends and visits them from time to time. His mother still lives as a refugee in Quetta, Pakistan, and, until recently, with his sister. Although she is now married and living in Australia. He still keeps in contact with me, and he still calls me 'teacher.' At Christmas in 2018, I received a parcel. It was a pair of buckskin trainers with a message: "Teacher, I give you these so you can walk with me some more." I treasure them still. He is the bravest of boys, learning to look forward and always walking with hope in his pocket.'
>
> (Volunteer English teacher, Kent)

Measuring distress

The World Health Organisation (2004), in its report about prevention, states that mental health disorders are a public health priority. The report links mental health to a human rights issue in the following way: 'Mental disorders are inextricably linked to human rights issues. The stigma, discrimination, and human rights violations that individuals and families affected by mental disorders suffer are intense and pervasive.'

Prevention is, therefore, a key priority in the care of all children, especially unaccompanied asylum-seeking children. As part of our Action Research learning with this cohort of children, we looked at measures that were being used in the local child and adolescent mental health services. None fit with the need to manage contextual distress, which so many of this group of children were experiencing (Bean et al., 2007), including Saad and Lidan, mentioned earlier in this chapter. We also needed a tool that supported us in managing any present and additional distress caused by being moved from one local authority to another, often to an unknown place on a map to be received by unknown people. We started to look at other areas of healthcare that understood contextual distress and were 'non-pathologizing' and discovered a *Distress Screening Tool* used in oncology.

In 1999, the National Comprehensive Cancer Network recognised that distress is associated with depression, anxiety, missed clinical appointments, and adverse treatment outcomes. In response, the Distress Thermometer was developed as a routine screening of distress for all cancer patients. The measure is a self-reported tool that uses a 0 to 10 rating scale. This has an additional prompt to be able to identify sources from which the distress is shaped via a problem list. The Distress Thermometer has been found to have adequate reliability in identifying clinical levels of anxiety and depression, compared to the Hospital Anxiety and Depression Scale (Knight et al., 2021). Ownby (2019) found that clinicians reported that, following training, the tool was easy to use and helped them to deliver appropriate psychological support. It also suggested a referral for additional support if this was indicated. The Distress Thermometer has an embedded, solution-focused process that is used to manage distress (Graham-Wisener, 2021). It is the first point of intervention when distress is present as part of the screening process.

In the world of psycho-oncology, there have been studies with international partners on aspects of distress in response to a cancer diagnosis and treatment. Studies have shown that the Distress Thermometer is clinically sensitive across cultures, as well as languages, worldwide. This validity meant that, with a cohort of children from all parts of the world, there was a proven sensitivity to its effectiveness in identifying distress levels (Lazenby et al., 2015; Donovan et al., 2022; National Comprehensive Cancer Network, 2020; and Graham-Wisener, 2021).

The *Distress Screening Tool* was developed and based on the Distress Thermometer. It was first described by us (Draper & Marcellino, 2020) as a 'non-pathologizing' tool, useful to assess the emotional health of young people and adults during times of potential distress. We published our first research (Draper et al., 2023) that indicated how, in a situation of ongoing trauma, the *Distress Screening Tool* had the efficacy to decrease the level of distress and capture any change occurring for a young person. It became the tool used by the National Transfer Scheme for every child being moved. It supports the child so that they have a shared decision-making process in the management of any distress that may occur. It enabled us, when transferring a child, to find ways to support and meet their distress needs. It also enabled those receiving a child to continue the support we had started.

'Martha used the Distress Screening Tool with a young person who was being moved to Watford. In the solution-focused process, she understood that he wanted to know more about Watford, where it was based, what it looked like, and what to expect. She showed him the geographical area on a map. They explored the history of the town and looked at Google Maps to see what it looked like. She made links to the fact that the Harry Potter studio was nearby and that the Elstree studios also often used the town for filming. He was able to look up a community within the town based on his own people and religion. He could see where the local mosque was based and who the imam at the mosque was. In the process of this, Martha was able to start the relocation process with Parwan before he had even left.'

(Martha, manager)

Table 3 An example of the *Distress Screening Tool* as used by a local authority for their looked-after children

Please circle the number that best described how much distress you have experienced in the past week including today.

Concerns list:

Family:

Bereavement.

Loss of contact with family.

Emotional:

Fear

Anxiety

Nightmares

Hypervigilance

Spiritual:

Loss of hope

Loss of peace

Loss of spiritual practices

Loss of spiritual community

Loss of choices

Physical:

Fatigue

Constipation

Sleep

Indigestion

Headaches

Extreme 10

9

8

7

6

5

4

3

2

1

None 0

Other and Self-reported most pressing concerns:

_____

_____

Competency based interventions:
0-5: Young Person does not require additional EM&WB support. Watch. wait and see protocol to be maintained.
6-7: Young person requires additional EH&WB support based on early interventions and seek consultation with Clinician.
8-10: Young Person requires additional EH&WB support and a review of any previous early interventions. referral to specialist services.

Solution Focused and Problem-Solving Process

Issue of Concerns:

Who/What is already helping:

Actions agreed:

For unaccompanied asylum-seeking children, the 'problem list' was modified to reflect issues that they reported were increasing their distress levels. These issues covered sleep, gastroenteritis, gastric reflux, headaches, loss of hope, bereavement, loss, etc. Essentially, the tool remained the same, yet the distress symptoms list was modified for this particular cohort.

The *Distress Screening Tool* does not see behaviour through the lens of a non-normative and complaint-based model, and there are no assumptions about what is normal or abnormal functioning (Fisch & Schlanger, 1999). It aims to understand behaviour as an aspect of ongoing social interaction (Fisch & Schlanger, 1999; Jackson, 1967). The solution-focused process is collaborative and co-constructivist (de Shazer, 1991). It is embedded in the *Distress Screening Tool* to support experiential and relational interactions. This enables the child to experience agency over their emotions and to learn how to manage distress and how to identify support systems that would enable them to reduce their distress. It is a shared decision-making process that, as evidence has shown, is an effective treatment (Montori et al., 2023). Using ideas from solution-focused therapy, along with narrative therapy, takes clinicians from a position of expert to being able to develop a more collaborative partnership (Nichols & Schwartz, 2008).

Dislocating episodes can affect young people's minds in terms of the level of distress shown, which can be associated with *dislocating* episodes. In the use of the *Distress Screening Tool*, it was showed that, to support the brain in accessing different neural pathways, there is a need to have repeated experiences that reinforce new pathways to be built.

Neuroplasticity is the brain's ability to change and adapt according to experience. This means that, regardless of age, it may be possible to rewire the brain and nervous system from the impact of transitions and critical moments. This can be helped to take place by having new, positive, and supportive experiences (Hanson et al., 2015). Neuroplasticity is, therefore, about creating new habits and experiences. There is a need to repeat the behaviours and experiences that we want to keep and to avoid the ones that we don't (Harvard Centre of the Developing Child, 2023; Tian et al., 2021; Lovering, 2022). The relationship between a child and others creates the interactions that continue to influence the brain's architecture.

A solution-focused approach (de Shazer & Berg, 1995) is embedded in the *Distress Screening Tool*. This tool is about an immediate response that is time-affected and is rooted in a willingness to do something different. In Kent, social workers, support workers, and reception centre staff used the *Distress Screening Tool* as soon as they met with the young person. It was a way to recognise that the *dislocation* taking place was distressing.

In the process of tracking the child's distress, there is an emphasis on what is changeable and possible. When a *dislocated* child is experiencing distress, their brain is highly likely to trigger well-known pathways that are about survival. They can feel stuck in this automatic response and find it difficult to do anything different (Copeland et al., 2007; Hanson et al., 2015).

> 'Girma would freeze. In those moments, when there would be tussling and playing with other young people, he couldn't cope with the free flow of activity. In the freezing that was happening, we would just let him be and continue to tussle and play together. It was about giving him space while not isolating him.'
>
> (Samantha, co-author)

What often happens is that the problem and the proposed solution are intertwined in a vicious cycle. From here, more attempts to manage the solution can lead to the persistence of the problem. This then leads to the same solution (Fisch et al., 1982). However, this can also be used to understand what maintains the problem and suggest what instead needs to occur next to resolve the problem.

> 'I was working in Romania with a woman who had been raped multiple times during the conflict. In the sessions, we talked about her bowel continually releasing faecal matter and the smell that this caused. We talked about the fact that her body was doing something to protect her by repulsing others from an area of her body that had been violated. Her body was reclaiming the sanctity of that area. Yet, it no longer needed to continue to do that. She reported that, in making this connection, her body had stopped releasing faecal matter as a way of protecting her.'
>
> (Juan, family therapist)

Some of the things that are triggering the distress will have solutions, while others may not. When the needs are not known to be associated with a transition or critical moment taking place, a solution-focused process can be employed in order to find ways to cope with and manage the distress being experienced.

> 'When I went to see Esta, she sat in the corner of her new room. I was told she had been there for hours. The noise in the new placement was unbearable for her. She told me how her memory of being imprisoned in her home country never left her mind, skin, body, and ultimately her soul. She would not tell me more. We sat and prayed together.'
>
> (Elisa, co-author)

The experience becomes about the potential we have to make change happen and manage the distress we are experiencing. It positions the child as an expert in their own life. A child ultimately knows what works for them and what they can and are able to do. It is in being alongside them, with lots of questions about the distress and what makes a difference, that new realisations can take place and solutions can be found. In supporting a child to develop their own distress management and solutions, they can start to embed this new pathway so that they can access solutions to problems or difficulties. This, in turn, reduces the distress they will experience.

> 'In our meetings together, Saab and I started to explore his stories of location. He described the best day of his life. He had been playing cricket, as this was his passion. He described the smell of the pads, the ball, and the sounds of the crowds watching him as he played. He told me that once he had hit a six, the ball had gone over the heads of the spectators. He could still see their faces

celebrating and cheering him on. The idea of playing cricket was the one thing that would bring Saab emotional relief. It created a sense of hope and purpose. It enabled a continuum of his ability as a gifted sportsman. To help Saab locate himself further, we contacted the local village cricket team and asked if he could play for them. They were delighted and welcomed him into their team. The staff and other boys from the centre came to watch. The village team actually started to win some games, and Saab loved the relocation taking place. Cricket had been what I had agreed to try and access as part of the solution-focused process embedded in the Distress Screening Tool.'

(Ana, co-author)

This tool helps us rate the level of distress from 0 to 10. It also has the ability to break down the distress through the problems list. As part of the process, it is important to consider future, distress-free possibilities. By doing this, a child can start to think about the plans they can make. They can also think about the people they can recruit to support them and the things that are needed to enable them to manage the critical moment and transition that is taking place.

We sometimes use questions such as the solution-focused 'miracle' question (de Shazer et al., 2007). An example of such a question is:

- If you woke up tomorrow morning and a miracle had happened while you were asleep, what is the first thing that you would notice that was better? What else?

Other times we offer a question that they themselves can use, a question that helps them identify their patterns of behaviour and the moments they have managed these patterns using effective strategies, for example:

- What do I do when my distress is high?
- When I was distressed before, what did I do, and what do I know helps?

There are also relational questions, such as:

- When I am experiencing distress, who could I ask for help?
- What would they say or do?

The solution-focused process facilitates a way in which, when there are transitions about to occur or a critical moment is on the horizon, a normalising of the distress that will be experienced can take place. In the collaboration, there is a coordination of intent. This holds the belief that the child can do something different, that they can tolerate distress, and that they can seek ways of managing the distress, for example, by asking someone to help them. This creates a virtuous cycle.

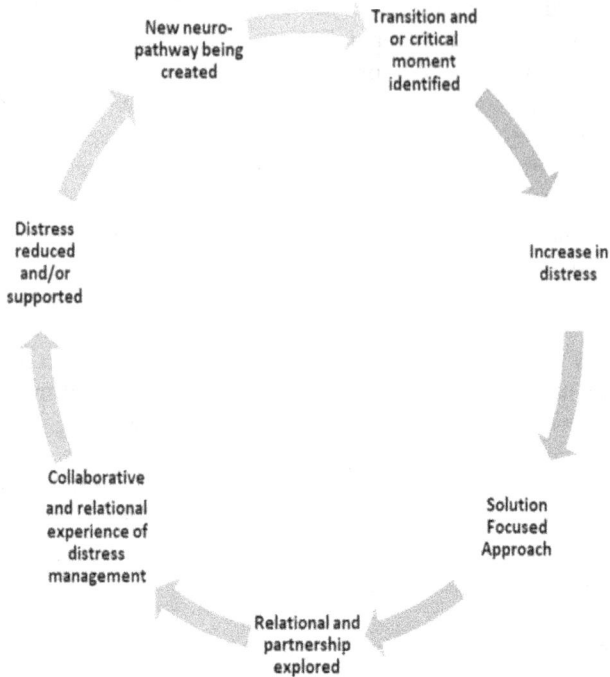

Figure 4.1 Here, we show the following key characteristics of this cycle.

It is in the repetition of this cycle that the experience becomes embedded as a new neural pathway. This supports the child to move away from past survival behaviours that could increase their vulnerability.

'Saab had been reporting that his distress was reduced when reviewing the Distress Screening Tool. Then he was told that he was about to be moved to Manchester, and his distress increased again. When we met, he talked about the transition about to take place and the loss of hope it created. We started to explore, together, what would give him hope. He named continuing to play cricket as a key resource that he wanted to have access to. I asked the cricket captain in the village if there was anything he could do. He wrote a letter of recommendation to a cricket team in Manchester and gave it to Saab to take with him. Another family from the village heard he was moving. They had seen that he was wearing borrowed whites and shoes from other members of the village team. They asked for him to be taken to the local sports shop so that he could have new whites and shoes to take with him.

The local authority, who would welcome Saab, was sent the Distress Screening Tool with all the work we had done together so that they could continue to support Saab. They would now have an understanding of his distress and the things that made a difference.'

(Ana, co-author)

The *Distress Screening Tool* was successfully implemented in Portsmouth (Draper et al., 2023). It was used to support unaccompanied asylum-seeking children as well as looked-after children in times of transition, such as when they were moving to a new local authority. It was also used at critical moments, including when they had an interview with the Home Office, their placement changed, or when they were being moved away from family. In a small study of this implementation, Draper et al. (2023) found that, of the 18 young people whose *Distress Screening Tools* were analysed in the Portsmouth study, there was evidence of distress being triggered by multiple stressors. These included going through the asylum process, changes in placement, and learning a new language, all descriptions of a *dislocating* process in which distress is a normal response. The study also showed promising results in reducing distress. There was a significant statistical difference between pre- and post-distress levels.

Danese (2019) describes the interacting, multiple adversities as leading to a cluster of symptoms rather than a specific disorder. They also describe that the more adverse the childhood experiences, the more extensive and overlapping are the emotional difficulties likely to emerge. These difficulties include anxiety, depression, self-harm, substance misuse, and disruptive behaviours. Yet, if we take distress seriously as a core concept for children who are undergoing and are likely to experience multiple adversities, we need to ensure that we support them to restore their well-being. We can do this by dealing with the distress through this type of transdiagnostic response embedded in the *Distress Screening Tool*.

'I remember Hamed going to London and sitting opposite me when we entered the tunnel. Suddenly, the train stopped, and the lights went out. I called out to him. "It's okay, Hamed." The lights came on, and Hamed was sitting statue-still, the blood had drained from his face, and tears were streaming down his cheeks.'

(Elisa, co-author)

We go on to describe other transdiagnostic responses that have been shaped by the voices of unaccompanied asylum-seeking children, the cluster of symptoms they experience, and the ways in which we can support them to *relocate* and thrive.

Outsider Witness reflection notes you may want to make about Chapter 4 are as follows:

- What in the chapter did I want to respond to the most?
- Is distress contagious? If so, how did it catch me?
- If I were to be curious about my own distress, what solutions would I find?
- Where are my head, my stomach, and my breathing when distress is present?
- When thinking about distress, how would I now describe *dislocation*?
- How will this change what I might, or might not, do next in my relationship with distress and in my practice?
- In witnessing my own distress, how do I now witness an unaccompanied child's distress?
- When I witness their distress, how do I want to respond?

Chapter 5

Sleep

With the sharp rise in sleep-related hospital admissions for those aged under 16 (Marsh, 2020), sleep difficulties have been described as a 'hidden public health problem.' Poor sleep practices have been linked to a range of functional impairments in memory, concentration, attention, motor performance, academic performance, and behaviour (Harvey et al., 2003; Pilcher & Huffcutt, 1996). Over 25% of children in the general population experience sleep difficulties within their early childhood years (Vriend & Corkum, 2011). Literature on sleep disturbances and effective interventions needs to be reflected in research on children's mental and physical health.

Rajaprakash et al. (2017) suggest that for children to develop and maintain healthy sleep practices, they require the support of parents and caregivers. As a result, sleep practices during childhood are centred around psychosocial and family factors. Therefore, it can be postulated that those who have experienced familial disruption and breakdowns during their early years are likely to experience higher levels of sleep disturbance. In line with this, research has found that young people who have lived in foster care are more likely to experience difficulties with sleep regulation (Tininenko et al., 2010).

Sleep is critical to well-being. It is fundamental to the base that needs to be in place from which a young person can thrive. In childhood and adolescence, there is a need for increased sleep as a way of enabling the body and brain to develop. The National Sleep Foundation (2022), following two years of research, breaks down the age range into nine age-specific categories. There is a slight range that allows for individual preference, as follows:

- Older adults, 65+ years: 7 to 8 hours
- Adults, 26 to 64+ years: 7 to 9 hours
- Young adults, 18 to 25 years: 7 to 9 hours
- Teenagers, 14 to 17 years: 8 to 10 hours
- School-aged children, 6 to 13: 9 to 11 hours
- Preschool children, 3 to 5: 10 to 13 hours
- Toddlers, 1 to 2 years: 11 to 14 hours
- Infants, 4 to 11 months: 12 to 15 hours
- Newborns, 0 to 3 months: 14 to 17 hours

DOI: 10.4324/9781003258681-6

Without the right level and amount of sleep, resilience is impaired, and young people are likely to experience fatigue, a short temper, and a lack of focus. In addition to these symptoms, there are also physical impairments. These physical impairments include a heightened likelihood of being obese, developing coronary heart disease, having diabetes, and having a shortened life expectancy.

Disordered sleep patterns also affect emotional well-being, with a higher likelihood of depression and anxiety disorders (National Health Service, NHS, 2022). Added to this, Gregory & Sadeh (2012) found that children and adolescents who had disordered sleep patterns also had attention disorders. This relates to an increase in diagnoses such as attention deficit hyperactivity disorder, with many of the symptoms of sleep deprivation being similar.

Another key physiological change that occurs when there is chronic sleep deprivation is the effect on appearance (Sundelin et al., 2017). Over time, this can lead to premature ageing and an increase in the body's production of the stress hormone cortisone (Vorona et al., 2005).

When the Sheffield NHS Trust piloted a cross-agency sleep behavioural intervention for vulnerable children, it found that there was a reduction in healthcare utilisation as well as illness and medication for participants. There was also an increase in well-being for the carers of these children (Elphick et al., 2019).

The child's environment was considered a key factor in their sleep hygiene (Hambrick, 2017). Tininenko et al. (2010) stated that sleep interventions could include routine assessments of sleep hygiene by foster carers. By *sleep hygiene*, we are referring to the creation of daily routines and sleeping environments that enhance the ability to have a regular and improved quality of sleep. Fusco & Kulkarni (2018) highlighted that sleep interventions may be more effective and accessible for young people as they are less stigmatising. Interventions should adapt a psychoeducational approach and inform young people how past trauma has affected their sleep.

> 'Whenever I stayed at someone's home or went away on holiday, I always needed to take my special teddy and pillow. This offered comfort and helped me get to sleep in a new environment. It gave some familiarity to a strange place. It relocated me to my own bed and environment.'
>
> (Samantha, co-author)

Unaccompanied minors may experience similar difficulties as looked-after and previously looked-after children (i.e. family disruption, maltreatment). Their difficulties may be heightened, as unaccompanied asylum-seeking children are a vulnerable group who are also exposed to continuous transitions throughout their migration trajectory (Bhugra, 2004). They may have experienced multiple traumatic events, such as imprisonment, persecution, and torture (Bean et al., 2007; Wiese & Burhorst, 2007).

Sleep intervention in the literature

There is limited research on sleep as a standalone difficulty as opposed to a symptom of post-traumatic stress disorder, particularly within the separated young population. If research primarily focuses on sleep as a symptom of post-traumatic stress disorder, how can interventions geared toward sleep difficulties not linked to it be considered in this population? As sleep difficulties have been linked to anxiety, depression, externalising disorders, and attention deficit hyperactivity disorder (Aronen et al., 2000; Benoit et al., 1992; Elliott & McMahon, 2011; Johnson et al., 2000), sleep must be considered an issue itself. This is to ensure that specific and effective interventions inform clinical practice.

It is well recognised in the literature that there is a relationship between nutrition, exercise, and sleep. A study that looked at sleep patterns with adolescents showed that there is a statistically significant link in respect to well-being when it is measured across all three factors (Awad et al., 2013).

Bronstein & Montgomery (2013) reported that unaccompanied minors' sleep onset latency was 20 minutes greater than what is considered a normative length of time to fall asleep. There was also a reported association between increased sleep problems and the presence of post-traumatic stress disorder. This included increased sleep onset latency, increased nightmares, and less total sleeping time compared with those groups not experiencing post-traumatic stress disorder. According to this study, the reactions of children were not necessarily specific to post-traumatic stress disorder; 77% suffered from anxiety, sleep disturbances, and/or depressed moods on arrival. Furthermore, sleep disturbance was primarily predicted when there was a family history of violence.

Lawrence & Michelmore (2019) undertook a rapid review of the research and literature. This was in respect of understanding sleep difficulties by both unaccompanied asylum-seeking children as well as children in care. They found that there was very little research in the area of care that linked sleep to a symptom of distress. Yet, in the findings, they were able to review and suggest that this cohort of children would benefit from sleeping in an environment that provided stability and security to promote good sleep. In addition, attention should be paid to the process of falling asleep.

'When I was a child, I used to wake up at night to admire the sea and catch a glimpse of the nearby beach through my window. In those moments, the world seemed to move in a slow time lapse. I could get to sleep almost instantaneously after.'

(Elisa, co-author)

Carr et al. (2017) found that the sleep work associated with the Action Research project in Kent was successful. Practitioners reported that it resulted in a significant improvement in sleep for young people. It also had a positive effect on their general health and well-being. The paper emphasised that the symptoms arising from sleep difficulties can be confused with signs of post-traumatic stress disorder. This finding was supported by Montgomery's (2011) review, along with the high prevalence of sleep disturbances reported in the studies. Montgomery points out that sleep disturbance is often not studied on its own. This is because it is only part of the diagnosis of post-traumatic stress disorder in young refugees.

Disordered sleep patterns, in response to interacting with multiple adversities, are part of a cluster of symptoms. As with distress, this requires a transdiagnostic response. In our experience of working with this group of children, it is only in the process of *relocating* that sleep patterns become normalised for the individual. Yet, when a new *dislocation* takes place, disordered sleep patterns revert. Therefore, any sleep interventions we do with a child need to be recursive, according to the critical moment and transition taking place.

'When Carim arrived at the reception centre, his sleep seemed not to have been affected by the transitions he had made on his arrival to the UK. He was waking up for breakfast and then going to the English classes that started early in the morning. He would enter into all the activities available to him. Yet, as the days progressed, he seemed more sullen. He was also less able to focus, confused, and, at times, almost like he was drunk. When I met with him, I asked him about his sleep, and he said he hadn't slept for many days, as he wanted to do the right thing and behave as expected of him. He had a sleep pattern, which meant that he normally slept during the day. Yet he had pushed himself to stay awake throughout the day.'

(Ana, co-author)

Montgomery & Foldspang's (2001) study highlighted the importance of family environment and a feeling of security in facilitating good sleep, following traumatic experiences related to war and violence.

The findings from these studies have relevant practice implications for how we work with unaccompanied young people. Firstly, young people, who are separated from their families, need, perhaps even more so than children with families, an environment that provides stability and security. This stability and security should aim to replicate elements of a family environment to promote good sleep. Secondly, attention should be paid to how unaccompanied asylum-seeking children manage the process of falling asleep. This is where one study found there to be a difference between other populations of young people. While this study included a large cohort, it primarily focused on refugees and unaccompanied minors from one geographical area. Therefore, more research is required into the process of falling asleep in unaccompanied minors from different countries.

Stories about sleep

The literature supports the findings of the Kent Action Research project, where children were complaining about their sleep patterns and their inability to sleep in a reception centre where they were staying. Additionally, young people reported the same difficulties once they were housed in the community. The move to a new home once again disrupted their sleep.

In local authority multi-agency meetings, there were reports of these young people having 'party houses' and that their sleep pattern was disturbing others in the local community where they lived. This was problematic for a number of reasons, including the fact that the young people struggled to access education. Also, their ability to link with and forge friendships with local residents was compromised. This vulnerability was also found to increase the risk of exploitation (Draper, 2016).

We noticed that the reception centre manager would, on a weekly basis, when there was a meeting that included everyone, complain that the young people would put towels over the lights, which was a fire hazard. She would request that they stop doing this due to the risks it created. This observation of risk due to sleep-related behaviours created an opportunity to explore sleep with the young people. This, in turn, helped us to further understand the disordered sleep patterns that many experienced.

Sleep became a subject of interest across the system, with education, social services, non-governmental organisations, and the National Health Service in collaboration. They all needed to explore ways of supporting these young people to gain the ability to sleep and to reduce the embedded sleep patterns associated with their migration journey. The local authority also started to talk about other looked-after, and previously looked-after, children who were experiencing disordered sleep patterns. They saw the need to support these children as well to gain a good night's sleep.

> 'When I met with the nurse lead of a children's home, he told me how he had used the framework. He discussed the sleep work and how staff would read the Harry Potter books to the young people before bedtime. "They never had this experience before, and no matter how old they are, they would sit on the sofa and enjoy the story."'
>
> (Elisa, co-author)

These conversations set up a further collaborative process. This process saw me (Ana, co-author) as the clinical lead, the mental health nurse, and the assistant psychologist, able to explore the stories children and young people told about sleep. Some of these stories are described further in the chapter, and the next story describes the interactions associated with sleep that took place.

> 'One interaction between staff and young people was the fact that lights were being left on overnight, yet coats were put over the lights to reduce their brightness. The reception centre manager kept asking the young people to stop doing this, as it was a fire risk. Yet they continued, reporting that they needed the light to orient when they needed to check where they were, yet the light was too bright and was prohibiting them from sleeping.'
>
> (Ana, co-author)

Reception staff described different ways of managing the difficulties experienced, such as introducing the sleep packs with night lights as a coordinated and relational response. It was a way to explore what might support these children in having an environment where sleep was more likely to take place.

When the project clinical lead came into the reception centre, she would notice children sleeping together in the lounge. They would huddle, with one child in the centre and others around him. They would hold each other as they slept. This was also a way of protecting those inside the huddle from unknown attacks and keeping warm during the journey. For these children, safe sleep was in the sound of another's breath; it was the smell and touch of them, as well as the heat they created in the closeness of holding each other.

Sleep was a complex interweaving of sleep patterns reflecting the need to travel under the guise of darkness and the hypervigilance associated with the need to guard against threats when asleep. This behaviour was to ensure survival. There was a need to support a change in this sleep pattern as they started to feel safe. The Action Research study found that the threat to well-being of *dislocations* taking place through transitions and critical moments would often reverse any progress a young person made in restoring their sleep. Therefore, the triangulated sleep interventions we went on to develop needed to become part of a continuum of care. It is from this new knowledge that sleep hygiene became part of the *relocation* tools required within the multiplicity of symptoms being experienced.

'I can't sleep in that room; it is the same shape and colour as the room that they held me in. I keep waking up expecting to be tortured. I have to get out of the room and try to breathe again. It's almost like it is happening again, and I end up choosing to sleep in the sitting room. This really annoys the people I live with.'

(Ahmed, unaccompanied asylum-seeker)

Ahmed is being *dislocated* in that the shape and colour of the bedroom he has been allocated remind him of the cell he was held in. He is actively trying to *relocate* himself by sleeping in the sitting room. This is seen as anti-social by the other young people he is living with. It was only when his room was changed to the colour of his choice and the bed was moved into a different position that he was able to reduce the distress caused by the associated *dislocation*. He was able to shift the *relocation* to his bedroom, as the bedroom became a place of familial colour and repositioned furniture.

Sleep in the action of discovery

The Action Research was supported by the following steps; these were taken in the participatory action from which new understandings about sleep emerged:

- To witness and hold the dilemmas described about sleep.
- To formulate an immediate response relating to the contextual events that impact their sleep.
- To develop a sleep hygiene PowerPoint presentation as a practical relational response. To continue to witness and hold the dilemmas being described about sleep.

- To develop sleep packs as a practical relational response. To further continue to witness and hold the dilemmas being described about sleep.
- To develop a circadian rhythm body clock. This enables a reset formulation and can audit outcomes for children in response to these steps of discovery.

Next, we use excerpts from short reports written as part of the Action Research project to highlight the learning that took place. We use the different voices that support an understanding of the sleep difficulties being experienced by unaccompanied children.

Notes made by the looked-after children's nurse, based at a reception centre, who continued to implement the *relocation* tools once the Action Research project had been completed, are also included.

Sleep hygiene support

Groups of young people were supported through a sleep hygiene presentation on arrival at a reception centre. One of the habits they had picked up on the journey to the UK was to drink lots of energy drinks. This, they reported, was a way of staying awake and alert to ensure their survival. Some young people reported drinking up to ten cans of energy drinks a day. This would have had a detrimental effect on their ability to sleep.

> 'Some of the young people reported that they had learned not to smoke before going to bed. Others reported that they didn't realise that the blue light from their phones might hamper sleep. While a number reported that they had been drinking high energy drinks and hadn't realised this might affect their ability to sleep.'
>
> (Andy, mental health nurse)

In supporting young people to have agency over their sleep hygiene, for example, not drinking high quantities of energy drinks, not sleeping during the day, not going on their phones late into the evening, etc., they were empowered to have control over their sleep in a way they hadn't experienced since arriving in the UK.

Anna, a reception centre manager, stated:

> 'The barrier of not sleeping is in their way. So, once they do start to rewire their body clocks, they do so well with the opportunities they take. This is because they are sleeping better.'

The migration that had taken place removed children from the aesthetics of sleep as they had once known it from a sense of *location*. It was therefore important to explore *locating* stories related to sleep.

Table 4 Dialogical communion from which relocation actions can emerge

Person speaking	What was said
Aarash:	'I just can't sleep; it is so hard to find a place where sleep works.'
Ana:	'There is something missing?'
Aarash:	'Yes, so much is missing; I am so alone; it's all wrong.'

Person speaking	What was said
Ana:	'When you say alone, what do you mean?'
Aarash:	'I have never slept alone before; I don't like it.'
Ana:	'When you were home with your family, how did you all sleep?'
Aarash:	'We slept on the floor together.'
Ana:	'Can you describe what it was like?'
Aarash:	'I slept next to my father; he slept next to my mother, who slept next to my sister, and the dog was next to me.'
Ana:	'So you were close in a room together; what could you hear, smell, and feel?'
Aarash:	'I could hear their breathing and felt the movements they made. They had a smell of belonging, of family, of being safe.'
Ana:	'If you were there, what else would you be noticing?'
Aarash	'I would hear the goat moving around and the chickens pecking. We were all in the house together.'
Ana:	'If your mum, dad, or sister were here, what advice would they give you about going to sleep?'
Aarash:	'They wouldn't understand what it is like to sleep alone. They wouldn't know what to say.'
Ana:	'Are the dog, goat, and chickens part of your family?'
Aarash:	'Yes, the dog always slept next to me.'

From a contextual perspective, I (Ana, co-author) needed to consider what could *relocate* Aarash to sleep. To enable Aarash to feel safe and *located*, his social worker looked for supported living, where there was a dog that could sleep next to him. It was a form of sleep hygiene bespoke to Aarash. It met his needs by creating an environment where sleep could happen. It *relocated* him to his ability to sleep and the experience of sleep he had previously had.

A professional who attended our training event for professionals who work with unaccompanied minors described the *Location, Dislocation, and Relocation* framework:

'I learned that early visual and practical items give more successful results, like an early acknowledgement that this is normal – that this happens to anyone who has experienced the things you have. It helped enormously in communicating the stories of others and their sleep difficulties. It is therefore important to explain and demonstrate sleep hygiene upon arrival in the UK.

'Stress balls – there were a variety of these. The young people preferred the stress balls with red hearts and the map of the world. I do feel that they wanted these to be displayed in their rooms rather than for their intended use. Maybe the world maps were a way of seeing the journey they had made, and the hearts were a reminder of the people they love.

'When we discussed nightmares, we explained that they occur because their brain is processing all that has happened. It is a sign of their ongoing well-being, which is managing what has happened before.'

(Reception centre nurse)

Sleep packs

Next, we describe how the sleep packs were co-developed with these young people.

> 'We all gathered together in the lounge and played with ideas of what might be useful. We then gathered again with things we had bought that could possibly support sleep. We brought night lights and showed how they worked, as well as sleep masks and worry dolls. They put in one of the boxes the best items they felt would help, and we agreed that in the following week we would make up sleep packs together so that everyone had one.
>
> 'The following week, they put the sleep packs together with the agreed items, and in the weekly group meeting that took place, they gave each other a sleep pack. For those who had recently arrived, they described the items and how they worked. The following week, at the same group meeting, we asked for feedback, and the feedback they gave was to stand, clap, and dance together.'
>
> (Ana, co-author)

As per the story about how the sleep packs were co-developed, the sleep behaviour of putting towels on the lights was information that was explored further. When questioned about this behaviour, the young people talked about needing some light to be able to check around them for safety. Too much light woke them, and they then struggled to go back to sleep.

Other stories started to emerge about noises that would wake them due to their hyper-alert state and the worry they had about family members from whom they had become separated or who were still back in their homeland. We explored with them the sounds and smells associated with sleep, and many mentioned the smells from plants that they missed.

> 'Eye masks and earplugs were important in the reception centre as people often came from the port at night. Again, I had to demonstrate how to use these and explain how they might be helpful.'
>
> (Andy, mental health nurse)

Slowly, it dawned on the team that a sleep pack, on arrival at a reception centre, may help in the following ways:

- Normalise the fact that sleep can be difficult on arrival and beyond.
- Create relational opportunities in the giving of the sleep packs.
- Support children to sleep better due to the aids in the packs.

At first, we struggled to get the items needed in the packs. As soon as we had packs, the young people would welcome them, and they would all be snapped up. The items in the packs that young people reported as useful were a night light, worry dolls, sleep masks, and earbuds.

We added a lavender bag and introduced this as the smell of sleep in England. The sleep packs were a way in which we were supporting children to *relocate* in the *dislocation* of arriving to a new country.

> 'In the first meeting with the young person, I always have a sleep pack with me. The most popular items included in the sleep pack are the night light and lavender bags. A young person told me that lavender reminded them of a similar plant back home. It was a smell that relocated him and helped him feel safe.'
>
> (Reception centre nurse)

As children arrived at a reception centre, we would ensure a part of the welcome for them was a sleep pack with information about what it was for and how they could use it. The first time we gave each child a sleep pack was in the once-weekly communal meeting. This is where we asked the young people to put the packs together and give each other a pack. The following week, we asked them if the packs had helped them sleep, and, as a way of communicating their delight, they stood, clapped, and danced.

> 'We promoted a culture where everyone participated in supporting and enabling sleep to happen. I promoted listening to music as well as reading, praying, thinking of good things, and remembering happy things. I encouraged everyone to implement these suggestions from dinner time, which took place at 5 p.m. onward. This helped them not to think about sad and worrying thoughts but rather to choose to engage in the things about home that aided sleep. One young person bought an herb plant that reminded him of home.'
>
> (Reception centre nurse)

Yet there was no budget for such a pack, and they were costing around £8.00 each. That is when the local community, under the guise of the 'King Singers,' held a concert to raise money. This enabled more sleep packs to be bought and used to support this cohort of children and young people.

These packs are now being used routinely to support unaccompanied children on arrival in the UK. The Separated Child Foundation, a London charity, supplies packs to local authorities as a way of ensuring that these are available for every child. Some local authorities have started to give packs to looked-after children, and a few adoption services also encourage new parents to create their own sleep packs to get their child ready for moving into their new home.

The reception centre reported that not one sleep pack had been left behind by a child upon moving into a new placement in the community. The manager stated that many things were left behind when children and young people moved to new environments, but never a sleep pack. It is as if they knew they would need it again in the transition they were making.

> 'I made sleep advice 'do's and don'ts' sheets from the relocation tools training to use when explaining ways to improve sleep. The sleep hygiene sheet was

laminated and available to them. They were then able to support me in understanding and meeting their needs accordingly. I documented all changes and
shared this with other staff to help maintain and support the change, as well as
to enable us to continue learning together.'

(Reception centre nurse)

Recalibrating the sleep pattern

The National Sleep Foundation (2022) describes circadian rhythms as 24-hour
cycles that are part of the body's internal clock. They run in the background to
carry out essential functions and processes. One of the most important and well-
known circadian rhythms is the sleep/wake cycle.

The sleep cycle can be interrupted by many things that may leave a child or
young person depleted. Children who experience multiple and continual Adverse
Childhood Experiences, through transitions and critical moments, are likely to
have this cycle interrupted. Without the right support, this is likely to become a
long-term symptom, especially as there is a recursive need to review the sleep patterns a child is experiencing.

The American Academy of Sleep Medicine has recommended chronotherapy
for the treatment of these types of disordered sleep patterns (Dore-Stites, 2017).
Chronotherapy is based on our biological response to light by restoring the body's
circadian rhythms (Cardinali et al., 2021).

'A young 17-year-old who was shy and timid, barely speaking to others,
greeted me one morning with the words, "I can sleep!" He had a broad grin
across the whole of his face. I had only worked with him for two or three
weeks. I asked him if he could tell the rest of the boys what he had spoken
about and what he did within the regular meeting, which took place with
young people and staff. I reassured him that I would be there to support him.
He could speak via the interpreter, to whom I would explain what we were
doing beforehand. Amazingly, he rose to the challenge and told the boys
what he had done and the difference it had made. In response, they gave
him spontaneous, rapturous applause. It was a wonderful moment both for
himself, as he was quite amazed, and for me. He told the other boys, "Rose
has helped me sleep. I can now sleep; listen to Rose."'

(Rose, community nurse)

In recalibrating a given sleep pattern, there is a need to ensure that the child has
support to create time for themselves in the sleep they are able to have to restore a
pattern of sleep that is linked to the individual's circadian rhythm.

'The whole of the reception centre started to get more proactive in their support
of getting children to sleep. It became a focus for all staff. Support workers were
taught how to use the sleep calculator. This is where they co-created, with young

people, prescriptions to support them in reversing their body clock. Girma was trying to follow his prescription, yet the struggle remained. He reported that his sleep was not getting better. In a review with Girma and his support worker, we discovered that he was getting up at 2 a.m. to speak to his mother every day. Neither of them realised the impact this was having on his well-being. Girma agreed to ask his mother if she could manage a different time so that he could get a block of sleep each night.'

(Andy, mental health nurse)

The sleep hygiene work was also helpful in stopping young people from getting up to smoke. The sleep packs also supported staff in managing the comings and goings caused by new arrivals in a reception centre. This optimised the possibility of being able to reverse the body clock issues that came with travelling at night and sleeping during the day, for safety reasons.

The staff ensured that a consistent message was being given about sleep. This helped young people prioritise their need to sleep within the centre. Slowly, a new culture of sleep started to emerge, and *relocation* became everyone's business. Posters were created in different languages about sleep. These posters were in the shared homes that the young people moved to. This whole system approach is described by Carr et al. (2017), along with the positive impact on children's health and well-being.

In developing this aspect of the sleep protocol, we focused on attempting to move a young person's bedtime and rising time each day around the clock until the delayed sleep pattern was rectified. For some young people, the sleep hygiene work supported them to make the changes themselves. As one of the looked-after children's nurses, based at a reception centre, says:

'I would tell them about the energy drinks and why they needed to stop drinking them. I mean, it made sense when you had to be vigilant and stay awake, but I would point out that they no longer needed to do that. So, they would stop drinking them, and their sleep got better, and they became happier. Sometimes it really was that simple.'

Yet other young people needed additional support.

'These children had slept in groups during the day and then travelled, once darkness fell, to avoid detection.'

The following algorithm was used to support a sleep calculator embedded in an Excel spreadsheet to create a bespoke prescription as required by any individual child:

- Normal hours of sleep in any given 24-hour sleep cycle
- Start time of sleep onset
- End time of sleep onset
- Date commencing sleep pattern shift
- 15-minute reversal every two days

By using chronotherapy, we worked on moving the bedtime by 15 to 30 minutes earlier each day, until the young person's body clock was on a normal schedule.

'Blood tests repeatedly revealed a vitamin D deficiency because of sunlight deprivation. In one young person's case, the three and a half months prior to his leaving Afghanistan had been spent in Taliban captivity, in an old house where tiny slits of windows were at ceiling height. Unable to see anything other than a slim slit of sky during those months, it was not surprising that his test results revealed a severe lack of vitamin D. The reception centre placed a row of chairs outside, and the vitamin D-deficient young people all had to sit there, in all weathers, to replenish their levels.'

(Izzy, volunteer teacher and advocate)

Another way recommended to help in the management of sleep difficulties is Bright Light Therapy (also known as phototherapy). The effect of the bright light is mediated through the eyes as the person sits in front of the lightbox, which propagates this light. Those using it should not stare at it directly but sit about 41 cm from the unit, which can be placed on a table at an angle (Levitan, 2005). It helps in managing circadian rhythm disorders. The time of exposure to the bright light, an artificial light, depends on each person's clinical presentation (Pail et al., 2011; Praschak-Rieder & Willeit, 2003). This therapy is implemented during autumn and winter and discontinued when there is a natural emission of light in spring and summer. Bright Light Therapy, when used, should be applied consistently on a daily basis to ensure its efficacy. It is important to work with different professionals to support this group of children, so that all aspects of the needs they present are backed up and managed in a coordinated and collaborative space.

Sleep deprivation is a form of torture, and many unaccompanied asylum-seeking children experience this form of deprivation. Aiding them to reclaim their ability to sleep is a significant act of resistance to the regimes they have fled and the ongoing *dislocations* they experience as part of their migratory process. It can be considered to be creating the possibility for justice – justice in action, and justice allowing for moving beyond sleep deprivation.

Outsider Witness reflection notes you may want to make about Chapter 5 are as follows:

- What is my own relationship to, and with, sleep?

Play with these questions as a way of exploring this chapter further:

- What does my body feel like when I am sleep-deprived?
- What are my sleep smells, sounds, and colours?
- What are my cultural stories about sleep?
- What impact has sleeping in different places had on me? How will this change what I might, or might not, do next in my relationship with sleep and in my practice?

Chapter 6

Nutrition and semi-starvation

Food is central to being fully human; it is a relational connector through which transformations can take place. In our eating together, we are sharing a sense of vulnerability. Yet, we are also creating belonging and, in those sharing moments, are able to connect.

If we don't look at the body, *dislocation* can take place. When semi-starvation has been a lived experience, then we are missing a key component from which well-being is made. We know that the evidence base around formulations in the management of anorexia and bulimia is that, during starvation, the brain is unable to function in a way that utilises cognitive abilities from which wellness can be enhanced. Why, then, do we not recognise that children who have experienced semi-starvation for prolonged periods are likely to require support in managing the physiological impact on their bodies?

Semi-starvation and its impact on the brain and body

It is important to understand the impact of semi-starvation on the brains of young people. This is especially so since unaccompanied minors often experience prolonged periods of starvation or semi-starvation. These needs should be addressed upon their arrival in the host country.

> 'We kept trying to feed him, trying to share meals with him, to make him feel safe and to feel the warmth of our care and welcome. Yet he ate really small amounts. I mean, I am an older man, and I ate so much more than he did. I couldn't believe he was surviving on such little food. He kept saying his stomach was full and he couldn't eat anymore.'
>
> (Foster parent)

In our work together with social workers, foster carers, and staff at the reception centre, we started to help each other make connections. These connections were between the amount a young person could eat at any one time and the need for frequent, small amounts of food. This way, we were supporting the process of a slow introduction of food by enabling the stomach to start expanding slowly.

DOI: 10.4324/9781003258681-7

Recent research indicates a direct connection between brain function and diet in the prevention and amelioration of mental health presentations (Ekstrand et al., 2021). Serotonin acts as a neurotransmitter in our brains. This helps to support good sleep as well as appetite and can regulate mood and contribute to the experiences we have of pain. A high percentage of serotonin gets made in the gastrointestinal tract, which forms part of the digestive system. Serotonin levels are impacted by good bacteria, which are key for our gut's health. This supports its microbiome by creating protection against toxins and bad bacteria, which, in turn, prompts the neural connection between the gut and the brain (Selhub, 2022).

> 'Jamal talked about the desert. Walking past the skeletons of people who had been before. The hunger and thirst as his body became desperate to move away from the heat and to eat the little bit of food that he needed to make last for days. He talked about the fear of being left by his traffickers. The fear that they would abandon him and leave him to die.'
>
> (Ana, co-author)

The impact of semi-starvation on our brain can be well understood by the Minnesota Starvation Experiment (Keys et al., 1950). This research was conducted in 1944 with 36 young adult males. In the first three months, they ate a normal diet, and then, in the following six months, they semi-starved (1,570 calories per day). The outcome of this study indicated that semi-starvation led to physical and psychological decline. This included a significant decrease in strength, stamina, body temperature, sex drive, and heart rate. In terms of the psychological impact, food became an obsession that they dreamed about, talked about, and read about. Their mental ability was noted to have decreased, although this was not corroborated by formal mental testing. Mood changes were also noticed. These included irritability, depression symptomatology, and general apathy (Keys et al., 1950).

> 'Yar lost the ability to manage. He was scared and angry, and he couldn't understand why he was being left behind and not given a new home. He felt confused and out of control. He didn't trust the social worker, who told him that it was just a delay because there wasn't a house available. Others had come and gone. Some who had arrived after him made him fearful. This sense of feeling unsafe was overwhelming. He scratched his arms, hit the wall, and barely ate. Now his stomach had shrunk from the semi-starvation that had already taken place on the journey he had made.'
>
> (Ana, co-author)

In the Action Research project, conducted in two reception centres, staff reported that the main presenting symptoms were disordered eating, self-harming behaviour, hopelessness, mood disorders (anxiety and depression), and an obsession with food (Draper, 2020). It was after hearing the young people's stories about semi-starvation that some other symptoms started to make sense. Among these symptoms were sleep difficulties, digestion difficulties, sensory hypersensitivity, headaches, dizziness, oedema, hair loss, reduced strength, intolerance to cold, paraesthesia, and a slow metabolism. These physical presentations can be mistakenly seen as only psychological rather than the effects of the experience of food deprivation.

'The GP, who came weekly to the reception centre, asked me to meet with Farci, who had come to see him at the clinic he hosted. Farci had been complaining about his heartbreak and the pain he was in. When I asked Farci about his heartbreak, he started to hold his heart. He then talked about the burning in his throat. I tried to ask him about the people he had left behind and the difficulties he might be experiencing due to the newness of arriving at the centre a week before. Yet he kept holding his chest and talking about the pain that was making his heart break and burning his throat. It was then that I realised he was talking about indigestion and reflux. This was something he was experiencing every time he ate.'

(Ana, co-author)

The practice nurse, who supported the GP in the clinic, undertook an audit of all the young people like Farci that they had seen at the centre. She found that the three main issues of concern for which these young people sought medical support were headaches, disordered sleep patterns, and gastric issues.

'I was always aware of the weight of the boys. They were skin over bone and looked so emaciated. The nurse said she couldn't use the body mass index to understand how underweight they actually were. Yet they were skeletal and would complain of being unusually cold. They would even wear coats in the centre.'

(Shona, support worker)

The body mass index has been devised as a way to measure height and weight, from which a healthy weight range is determined. This measure was developed in Western society, in which the height and weight norms were determined by a Caucasian population. In using it outside of that population, there is a risk of error, as the height and weight range are different within other ethnic groups. When we eat foods that contain vitamins, minerals, and antioxidants, the brain is supported and nourished. This enables a reduction in the development of oxidative stress. These are all unwanted substances that are produced, causing damage to the cells. Research in this area has shown that foods containing large quantities of refined sugars can reduce the way the brain functions and decrease mood. This can lead to mental health conditions like depression.

The ecology of food: stories of cultural location

There are many cuisines around the world, as people from different cultural backgrounds eat a variety of food. Also, the preservation techniques, methods of preparation, ingredients, type of food, and type of presentation of food vary among cultures. The role and meaning of food are complex and vary among individuals and communities.

> 'Every time I go back home to Italy, I bring back coffee. No coffee smells like the one I have known since I was a child. Mum used to make coffee for everyone in the morning. That coffee smells like home; it smells like family.'
>
> (Elisa, co-author)

Food conveys different identifications that can be associated with many of the Social GGRRAAACCEEESSS (Burnham, 2012). The most important are gender, ethnicity, religion, culture, and class. When considering ethnicity and culture, foods are likely to become more significant when someone is not in their home country.

> 'Matty, my brother, and his boys would tell stories of the times they were able to go to the Ecuadorian restaurant in London and eat patagones and hornado together. James found an Ecuadorian food shop and gave us all guava jam for Christmas. At our Christmas celebration together, Granny B would always make her 'pregnant' rice, which was an all-time favourite. It was a twist on Ecuadorian rice, as lots of vegetables were added. A side dish of aji criollo was always nearby. This made the dish come alive for most family members.'
>
> (Ana, co-author)

People's tastes are recognised from birth; therefore, people are used to certain textures that are maintained later in life (Forestell & Mennella, 2015; Steiner eal., 2001). This influences our dietary choices and behaviour throughout life (Glanz et al., 1998).

> 'When, on holiday in India, a meal was served on a banana leaf with Thali dishes, cutlery was not offered. The custom was to eat the food with the left hand by mixing the curry into a paste with the rice. From a Western cultural perspective, this felt totally alien and reminded me of being a child and learning to eat with a knife and fork. My mother would tell me off if I did not do this tidily or use my fingers to help me. In a different cultural context, there was a permission that this was okay, which was different from the culture I grew up in. This brought a sense of dislocation and discomfort.'
>
> (Samantha, co-author)

This sense of *dislocation* is often mirrored by unaccompanied minors when offered food that is on a plate with a knife and fork.

Cohen (2021) described how religions have different rules about food and fasting. They have rules about what food is acceptable, who can eat it, and when. He described how food practices provide an understanding of religions and why people act in certain ways around food, considering their status, hierarchy, gender, etc.

'Girma wanted to fast; it was a new thing for him since going to the Eritrean church. He ate vegan food for several months in a row. His foster mother would try to cook for him to ensure that he ate well. However, she struggled to always understand his fast and when he had to do what. Slowly, they both got better at knowing what to do and would celebrate the end of the fast by going to an Eritrean restaurant. Girma would laugh at his foster mother's inability to eat with her hands. She would also pull faces at the bitterness of the bread and make several faux pas when it came to etiquette. Here, the shoe was on the other foot; he knew – she didn't. He would teach her, just as she had taught him, how to use a knife and fork.'

(Ana, co-author)

Examples of such teaching would include the preparation of pork, gelatine, halal meat, and kosher foods. There are also religious celebrations such as Ramadan and Yom Kippur, where fasting is practised, and a vegan diet needs to be understood.

'A foster parent was thinking about the diet of an unaccompanied minor she looked after. She shared with us that they ate very little of the food she offered. This was a frustration for her. Their only eating pleasure came through a brand of takeaway burger and chips on a Saturday. This would remind them of his family's ritual before leaving his home country.'

(Andy, mental health nurse)

In this description, there is a willingness to understand the meaning of different foods for a young person and how this links to the present. It is a way in which *relocation* is taking place through the reconnection to a ritual of a type of food eaten at the same time each week.

Food as relational

Food has a symbolic meaning with significant sensorial associations that run deep through our bodies. Cooking and eating are shared human activities, perhaps some of the few that can be said to be truly universal (Parasecoli, 2011). Cooking can evoke memories and be communicated to others, including the therapist, through the powerful imagery of food.

'In my family, when things were difficult for any member, we created a ritual of a 'bittersweet' meal. We would make sweet and sour vegetables, and as we ate them, we would talk about both being human and being fully alive. We would explore the sweetness and how it blended with the sour to make a symphony in which we could experience tastebud heaven. It was a way of holding each other in our success. It was also a way of holding each other through some of the difficult things we experienced as a family.'

(Ana, co-author)

In the article 'The Repercussions of Baked Beans,' I (Ana, co-author) share the story of a young child who was unable to eat the baked beans on toast that her nanny had made for her Draper (2012). She would become angry when it was placed in front of her and would throw the plate across the room. When this was explored, the young child said that her mother had always cut up the toast for her. She further explained that every time her nanny made it for her and didn't cut the toast, it would remind her of her mother's death. In response, she would experience anger as an acute moment of grief. The anger was a response to the *dislocation* taking place in the loss of ritual and routine, which, in turn, was embedded in the act of preparing and eating a meal.

Eating food is a marker of identification. It has a particular collective identity. The rituals surrounding food and meals provide opportunities for demonstrating to others the richness of one's culture. They also show one's own skills in the preparation of food (Beagan & Chapman, 2012). As food is so central to our lives, it has always been used in religious rituals (Fox, 2003).

'Not long after arriving at a reception centre, Esmat wanted to start Ramadan. His sleep and eating were already disordered, and we had been working with him to support his body clock reversal. Yet, his need to end the long journey he had made with the holy ritual of Ramadan was something we recognised together. It was a way in which he could relocate in the present. This was more important than anything else in marking the horror of the journey he had completed. It was also important for his wellness and ability to participate in making, both concrete and real, this aspect of his journey's end.'

(Ana, co-author)

When we talk about food, we link it to aspects of our identity. As therapists, it is important to be aware of our own relationship with food and how it might impact the perspective we bring to our work with young people. This includes our own beliefs and cultural relationship with food. How, as clinicians, can we be mindful of the ways we talk about food to avoid moralising and labelling it as 'good' or 'bad'? Sometimes what we define as 'bad' could be a *locating* food for a young person.

'When I was working with a young girl who had been adopted, her mother would collect her and take her to McDonald's straight after the session. This is something her child requested from her, and it became a ritual each week. I became curious about this ritual, and I started to ask the young child what she liked about McDonald's and why she wanted to always go there with her mother after our sessions. She told me the story of only seeing her birth mother when she wasn't high or drunk in a similar setting. She wanted to relocate herself to the mother who had talked with her, held her, and fed her, just for those few times, before she walked away with her 'now' mother. She wanted to relocate with her 'now' mother after talking with me about the dislocations that had taken place.'

(Ana, co-author)

When we think about resources and tools from which *relocation* can take place, we need to retain curiosity at the centre of our conversations. We also need to ask *located* questions. We would encourage you to first practice by asking yourself the following:

- What senses are most involved in food for me?
- What food reminds me of past experiences?
- How would I describe my relationship with food?
- What kinds of foods do I have a sensory preference for? Soft or crunchy? Creamy or spicy? Hot or cold?

'Mum used to prepare a delicious apple cake for us when we were younger. She never liked baking and preferred cooking. However, she knew we all loved cakes. So, on special occasions, she would bake the apple cake for us all. She would make four of them at once! I still remember the smell, the oven on, the music in the background, the flour on the table, and her smile whilst she was making something for her children, for us.'

(Elisa, co-author)

These questions are about being curious about what *locating* foods look like, taste like, and feel like. They are about food as a resource from which comfort can emerge. The Action Research project published an information book about the need for this type of *location* called *Comfort Food*, which expands the idea of food being a 'duo-biography' from which *relocations* are created (Draper, 2012). Duo-biography refers to the co-existence of two identities, one in the past that is brought into the present.

Because food is relational, it can be used as an act of resistance. Sometimes young people want to express their distress through the powerful act of total voluntary fasting.

'Fariad was on a hunger strike. This was his third day, and although he would drink water, he refused to eat anything until he was allowed to be reunited with his brother. In our conversation together, he talked about the strike being the only way in which he could gain a sense of control and be heard. The strike was his way of shouting his dissent at the continuity of being separated.'

(Ana, co-author)

Fariad is not the first person to show his dissent by not eating. In some societies, this type of total voluntary fasting is used to bring attention to an injustice as a way of shaming the powerful. It is a powerful act of protest and resistance against a situation in which someone has no control.

Continuing Bonds Enquiry: cooking as an act of remembering

'Recipes of Life' is a narrative, therapeutic concept developed by Natalie Wood (2012) with the intent to integrate talking therapy with cooking and eating sessions. This is a way to allow conversations about identities, values, and bonds to emerge in a different setting – the kitchen. There are, in fact, many stories left untold and invisible in the therapeutic room. These include stories that are deeply connected to a person's identity. In this sense, food represents a universal language that is both safe and accessible. It is a source of rich metaphor and symbolism where stories can be shared.

The act of cooking and eating brings a collective memory component as recipes are passed on from one family member to another. Food also brings a sensory and visceral element. The sensory experience connected to food can be extremely evocative of memories (Holtzman, 2006). It connects our personal experiences to our culture. Generations upon generations have listened to the origins of recipes and their culture, all while preparing and sharing food.

> 'Zahir, a 16-year-old boy, was referred due to anger management difficulties. His parents were from Ghana and moved to the UK when he was a young child. Zahir's mother died from illness when he was 10. In our sessions, Zahir had spoken about the importance of his relationship with his mother. He described his mother as a lovely and warm parent and a great cook. The therapeutic work was looking to create the possibility of sharing special moments and connecting in new ways with his mother. So, questions about what meal most reminded him of his mum were asked. Also, if he remembered the first time he tasted the meal, what made it his favourite? When did his mum cook it for him? And what does this food mean to him? We also explored the ingredients of life that make this meal special for him. These included love, optimism, and faith. Here, he spoke about how and when some of these ingredients came into his life. These ingredients were homegrown by his mother and went back to his ancestors. They were his family's heritage and legacy. We then talked about any tips or techniques that could have been left by his mother; he said, "Cover it and let it remain in a safe place for the time needed," a tip he could also use when feeling angry at himself and the world. His mother's wisdom and knowledge of him were brought into the present through her recipe.'
>
> (Elisa, co-author)

'We started to have 'comfort food' sessions, with the translator giving the boys the recipe for their favourite meal. They would buy the food, and she and I would go to their house and support them in learning to cook the meal together. As we ate together, I asked Abel who had last cooked this meal for him. He then told the story of his mother cooking him his favourite meal, one that they shared together as a family. He said the food was a reminder of her love for him. He was delighted that now he could cook it and feel close to her when he ate it.'

(Andy, mental health nurse)

Relocation tools

The *relocation* work around food is based on an understanding of the body-mind connection, starting from the vagus nerve.

Browne (2021) helps us understand this complex biology by describing the vagus nerve as a 'superpower' in the body.

The vagus nerve provides the brain and the gut with information about the wellness of our organs (Breit et al., 2018) by maintaining the immune and digestive systems as well as the cardiac rhythm (Waxenbaum et al., 2022). Furthermore, it helps with mood regulation and connects to how we manage more negative feelings of stress, anxiety, and fear. This can be referred to as our 'gut feeling.' It can be used to reduce the effect of the fight or flight responses by increasing our ability to access a healthier response to traumatic events. This enhances resilience.

A healthy vagal tone can be activated through the use of meditative exercises, especially yoga, that are beneficial for regulating breathing (Tyagi & Cohen, 2016). Yoga can stimulate the vagal tone and has been found to be beneficial in reducing post-traumatic stress disorder (Descilo et al., 2010). A relationship between vagal tone and diet impacts how much we eat. It also regulates weight (Tschöp et al., 2000).

Our throats are used as the passage from which we feed and are fed – as a way of sustaining ourselves. Mothers, as they nurse their babies, will sometimes sing or make tonal noises in their throats. This is a way of soothing the baby during the feeding.

'As I held my baby to my body and fed him, I felt his warmth on my skin. This skin-to-skin contact bonded us. I stroked his cheek and sang him a song about him being 'my sunshine.' This was the same song that played on the radio while I was pregnant. He would have heard it as he bathed in my womb. In those moments of feeding, he would often relax into a sleep; it was as if he melted into the smoothness of his milk.'

(Samantha, co-author)

The vagus nerve is key to the benefits of intuitive eating, which, in turn, promotes the recognition of the cues in our body for hunger and fullness. Intuitive eating was found to reduce disordered eating. This is because it removes the psychosocial pre-concept around what is 'good' or 'bad' food (Linardon & Mitchell, 2017). It works on improving one's relationship with food by reinforcing the connection between body and mind. It provides a sense of agency over how much and when food is needed (Linardon & Mitchell, 2017). When we redirect a person to get attuned to their internal cues, they understand when they are full or hungry. This is preferable to relying on an external source when they want to lose weight, such as a rigid diet.

Research also found that intuitive eating improves emotional distress and psychological adjustment. It is connected with lower rigid control and a healthy body mass index (Tylka et al., 2015). Linardon & Mitchell (2017) discussed, in their research, how intuitive eating could promote public health and prevent eating disorders. Body image acceptance is linked to intuitive eating, greater self-compassion, and higher emotional functioning (Schoenefeld & Webb, 2013; Bruce & Ricciardelli, 2015).

There are some live bacteria and probiotics that have been researched and investigated in the past decade. These bacteria are now well known to support the health of our gut (Shahrokhi & Nagalli, 2023) and improve the immune system, as well as improving bowel movements (Khalesi et al., 2019). Probiotics create a balance between the good and bad bacteria that support body functioning (Fuller, 1989). These bacteria also promote cognitive functioning and reduce mood disorders by decreasing stress levels (Kim et al., 2021). Due to their benefit to mental health, they are also known as psychobiotics (Del Toro-Barbosa et al., 2020).

Hunger-body-mind connection: cue profiling

The ability to understand and recognise the subjective cues from our body is known as interoceptive awareness. This includes signals from different parts of the body, for example, the gastrointestinal, cardiovascular, and respiratory hormone systems (Culbert et al., 2016; Khalsa et al., 2019). A study, completed on 200 university students, found that those who were hungry had more unpleasant emotions compared to those who focused on how they were feeling beyond the hunger signals (McCormack & Lindquisk, 2019). When the mind is attuned to emotion beyond the body's need for food, it can differentiate emotion from hunger. This, in turn, could have an impact on our long-term mental health and our understanding of what is linked to different aspects of our well-being.

> 'The whole family was in meltdown. Each had been in their own space of individual need, yet not connecting to our bodies' need for food. We were sniping at each other, getting more and more disconnected as our bodies started to manifest the need for food in the emotions we were having. We were all becoming 'hangry' and desperately needing to find food that would support us to reconnect.'
>
> (Samantha, co-author).

This research links to other findings from clinical trials where starvation was a key feature in anorexic patients. In these trials, there was evidence of lower interoceptive awareness and the ability to recognise hunger cues (Khalsa et al., 2015). Cue profiling helps a young person understand what cues their body gives them so that they know that they are hungry.

These cues may include:

- **Stomach:** rumbling, gurgling, gnawing, emptiness, aching, nausea.
- **Throat and oesophagus:** dull ache, gnawing.
- **Head:** cloudy thinking, light-headedness, headache, difficulty focusing and concentrating, increased thoughts about food and eating, especially craving high energy foods.
- **Mood:** irritability, crankiness, increased effort to stop oneself from snapping.
- **Energy:** waning, sleepiness, lethargy, dullness, or apathy in doing anything.
- **Temperature:** increased sensitivity to cold, feeling cold, especially in hands or feet.
- **Sensory symptoms:** increased sensitivity to noise, light, smell, touch, or taste.

When using this understanding as a *relocation tool*, we are actively supporting awareness of interoceptive abilities, for example, differentiating hunger from thirst. This attunement to a sense of being *located* in our body and connected to its function and abilities shifts the *dislocation* that is happening to their physiology. This is in response to the *dislocations* that have taken place. Some of the young people have experienced being raped multiple times on the journey they have made. Here, the association with their bodies being controlled and defiled could become linked to eating food.

> 'Malik's throat was sore from the gastric reflux that kept rising and burning. He had no control and could not stop the soreness from what he came to associate as the poison his body was removing from the food he ate. It was like a foreign body that needed to be removed. It got to a point where he started to eliminate it by putting his fingers down his throat. That way, there was no burning, and he had control. He would remove the foreign object from his body. He could retain control.'
>
> (Ana, co-author)

We encourage these young people to engage in regular check-ins. This is so they look to spot these bodily cues and respond to them. In addition to this, enquiries about what type of food they would like, i.e. soft or crunchy, warm or cold, etc., can be made. That said, for some young people, a regular check-in may feel invasive and controlling. As part of the *Distress Screening Tool*, it is important to find a solution-focused way in which these tools can be used. This is to capitalise on brain plasticity to enhance new pathways.

> 'I had to relearn how to eat when I was hungry. I had to start to notice what my body was saying, rather than the things my brain told me about my body. I started to trust myself more, to know that I could be in tune with myself rather

than in control of myself. The more control I tried to have, the less I had, and the worse my eating got. I would starve, then binge, then starve again. It was like I was on a swing, sliding from one excess to the next. I had to remind myself that I could trust my body to be what it needed to be. I started to understand the lies I had been told. I then told myself they were just that, lies. They were no longer what I had to believe or needed to keep telling myself.'

(Duka, young person)

This connects with emotional regulation work and how food is one way of making sense of emotional responses. When thinking about emotion and food, we need to be curious about our bodies' agency and autonomy. For example, I can feed myself when I want and when I am hungry. I don't need to hide or hoard food to notice the difference between hunger and the emotion that is being experienced.

'Between lessons at the reception centre we had a coffee or tea break. Eritrean boys love milk and would often choose a massive cold milk drink rather than a hot beverage. As I waited, a scuffle broke out in the queue just ahead of me. A new, but painfully thin boy watched as the Eritrean in front of him emptied the last of the milk into his cup. The boy immediately in front of me literally screamed and tried to get hold of the boy with the full cup of milk. "No more milk, no more milk." I jumped in between the boys and told them, "There is always more milk; don't fight; come with me." Together, we took the boy to the kitchen and showed him the fridge with extra milk. In that desperate moment, I was reminded that unaccompanied asylum-seeking children had experienced long queues, waiting for food dispensed by the World Health Organisation and other agencies, from the back of lorries. He had heard the cry, "No more milk, no more food; come back tomorrow," and he had been hungry. He knew that tomorrow didn't always come. So many of the young people had stomach problems resulting from a lack of food or clean water. There have been days without food or water, and boys are exhausted and near starvation.'

(Izzy, a volunteer teacher and advocate)

Yet, in the management of these symptoms, we can also help *location* stories emerge. We can also help *relocation* possibilities to be present as resources. These resources can enable well-being in an ongoing relationship with food.

'We sat and gathered together. We ensured the kindness of a welcome from the community at the heart of the reception centre, who had been invited by these unaccompanied boys to be part of their Eid al-Fitr. They sang and danced, and we clapped to the rhythm of their sounds. Then, we shared a meal that they had helped prepare. In the sharing of that meal, we celebrated the gift of our similarities and differences. We acted as witnesses and shared together the celebration of this ending of a fast.'

(Gladys, Kent Kindness volunteer)

A social worker told me (Ana) that children enter into care underweight and leave overweight. Children and young people who have experienced multiple transitions and critical moments, we would suggest, are more likely to have experienced semi-starvation as a bodily *dislocation*. Understanding the impact of this and how it connects to an ongoing process with behaviours linked to the experience of semi-starvation is critical. Food is a powerful *relocation* tool from which body and mind connections can be made.

Outsider Witness reflection notes you may want to make about Chapter 6 are as follows:

We invite you to reflect on your own relationship with food. The following questions are also useful reflections as part of the witnessing work you are undertaking around food:

- What 'sense' do I make of these food ideas in response to different aspects of who I am?
- Who has fed me, and how?
- If I were to name the best meal I ever had, what would I say it was?
- What does a full or empty stomach mean to me?
- Who do I share meals with, and how do we eat together?
- Think of a festival where food has been eaten; what meaning does it give to the food?

Chapter 7

Continuing Bonds Enquiry

A starting point for an enquiry

In an article we wrote about the *Continuing Bonds Enquiry*, we started by thinking about the cultural perspective from which we understand the different beliefs and customs that are associated with death and loss. Every country and society have their own beliefs and understandings of what it is to be human and to be a society. Many of these beliefs stem from a variety of sources, such as religion and political and geographical influences. These can be linked to a colonisation of people within the inter-relational interactions that have taken place.

Colonisation is the negation of time; it is about depriving someone of their story, culture, and faith to be replaced by that of the coloniser. Machiavelli (1953), known as the father of modern political philosophy and science, saw history as the repeated deletion of human memory.

> 'Sometimes I would catch myself trying to find my adopted sister. I would look for her among strangers walking down the street. My heart would pound and, in a fleeting second, I would think, "There she is!" Then I would realise that it wasn't her, and I would lose her all over again. I would also find her in my dreams. She would be brushing my hair and then laughing as she hugged me. Then I would wake to find myself in England in a cold house in the snowy rain – without her, as if she were deleted.'
>
> (Ana, co-author)

Unaccompanied asylum-seeking children are not without a past and a history; rather, they are people *located* outside of time (Mbembe, 2021). In Nietzsche's theory (Grimm, 1979), time has a circular structure, much like a clock face. Time, for him, possesses the topological properties of a circle; it is infinite and unbounded. He claims that everything will return to us, even this moment. Therefore, all temporal entities, such as events and moments, are both before and after themselves in time. So history, in the form of lived moments, will occur again as part of a circle of events. As Bakhtin (1993) puts it, no one can predict the future through the past, as the past changes all the time.

DOI: 10.4324/9781003258681-8

An unaccompanied asylum-seeking child's identity and story are often questioned and disregarded, therefore untold and unknown (Pearce & Pearce, 1990). Their only identity is understood in terms of the things they have run from – the wars and massacres, the human rights violations. Being an asylum seeker is the only story known about them. Migration is a catalyst through which a person experiences multiple changes, such as the loss of cultural norms, religious customs, and social support systems (Bhugra & Becker, 2005). In our work, we need to consider the colonisation that takes place for this group of children. These multiple changes are likely to impact perceptions of self and identity. This may create a process similar to that involved in the grief associated with multiple losses, from which a colonisation of the individual takes place. Their grief can only be performed within the accepted religious, cultural, and linguistic norms of the host society. It is a form of *dislocation* from the expression of grief that is *located* and ritualised in different aspects of their identity. It is only in the *relocation* that they can reclaim language, rituals, and cultural expressions from which their grief can be expressed.

We also need to consider how we can form acts of resistance. We can do this by ensuring that our enquiry is about rediscovery, mourning, dreaming, commitment, and action. Each of these is linked to the steps of decolonisation that need to continue to take place (Laenui, 2000).

When we think about these steps, we need to understand what each step is, as well as how it is made and what happens when it is made. This is not linear but rather a circular process in which time is in the past, the present, and the future.

The rediscovery of a child's history and the recovery of culture, language, identity, and religion are seminal in the steps that need to take place. A key issue for unaccompanied asylum-seeking children is the narrative about age. Age, in different cultures, is calculated by different calendars, such as the lunar calendar in the Islamic world. Yet, only the Western understanding of age is permitted with the associated roles and responsibilities of the individual.

Mourning can happen at any time in the cycle when a loss becomes present and is in response to the rediscovery and recovery that have taken place. In the asylum process, we prolong the mourning taking place. We do this by reducing the ability to tell a full story from which other aspects are known, told, and heard. Therefore, mourning becomes a perpetual state of being. This is because there is stagnation caused by the only story that they can tell, that of being an asylum seeker.

Whenever we enquire about dreaming, we are exploring the future, which usually consists of hopes and possibilities. From this point, new ways of being and becoming can both be a link to the present while also being embedded in the past and future. This also connects to the idea that the enquiry time is ever-shifting and not linear. It is also important to determine whose dream it is, who first had the dream, and what the dream looks like in the present and future.

When we previously wrote about the *Continuing Bonds Enquiry* (Draper et al., 2022), we told the story of Hussain and how his dream was articulated through his mother's hope through the act of helping him escape.

Hussain linked a new idea, from the present, to the hopes his mother had for him. In doing this, he created a bond with learning English through the enquiry we had together. He dreamed of speaking English as a way of holding hope. His mother's voice is his family's history. It enabled him to find a direction in which the commitment to learn English became something that belonged to him and his mother. This is articulated when the therapist asks, *'So, hope is yours and hers every time you say something in English?'*

Hussain's selfhood lies in the act of speaking English. It is his commitment, his history, and his story. In this cycle, he can start to recover from his dependence on being told that he is an asylum seeker. From here, his fixed identity, much like a noose around his neck, is loosened. He joins Alex, the person who told his own history at the beginning of the book and said, 'Today I am held, and I hold you by sharing my steps to success': the very steps of decolonisation that need to continue to take place (Laenui, 2000).

Alex and Hussain create what, in essence, is a cultural memory. This ensures a 'textuality of the past' in the experience and, therefore, a conscious memory of being an unaccompanied asylum-seeking child. This creates a stabilisation in their self-image, which conveys collective shared knowledge (Ibler, 2019).

As mentioned, history has many examples of ways humanity has tried to erase the past. However, the importance of the past is indisputable, as, in the past, lies our identity, the answer to the question, 'Who are we?'. Time is a powerful theme in therapy, and it is embedded in the *Location, Dislocation, and Relocation* framework.

In reinstating the past there is a re-connection, a touching and being touched by echoes, repeats, and fragments. The individual storage of the past is to be revisited and reused.

'The wonderful guard, Charlie, was processing a newly arrived young Afghan boy. I kneeled down and spoke in Dari/Farsi. "Peace be to you; you are safe, and I welcome you." He looked up, and it was the child I'd seen on the news the day before. Charlie told me, "He's exhausted, but stay with me until I've processed him." The boy had a black bin liner, and Charlie shook its contents out on the floor. He had a small broken comb, a stone, and a scrap of thin black material no bigger than a postcard. Charlie motioned to his clothes and asked the boy where his clothes were. The boy gestured that what he was wearing was all he had. Yet, I was curious: what were those three random items that he had carried with him on his journey to the UK? The stone, possibly a prayer stone, was clearly something precious to him – a piece of home. The scraps of thin black fabric, torn from the clothes of someone. From my time in Iran, I guessed it was the fabric of a woman's chadda, or veil, a remnant of someone dear who had been left behind. These were important memories from home.'

(Izzy, volunteer teacher and advocate)

This Afghan boy's black bag and its contents, like the small broken comb, a stone, and the scrap of thin black material, create a stabilisation of identity from which he has breath. In the re-connecting, he is beyond time in that the representation of someone dear is present despite their absence. This is a bond that connects, strengthens, and reduces the sense of being alone.

It is from stories like this that we started to connect to Klass' idea of Continuing Bonds (Klass & Chow, 2011). We started to think about our own acts of resistance to the colonisation taking place and how we can 'enquire' rather than 'inquire.' In enquiring, we are taking a curious position from which we are in a mutual process of discovery. Inquiring instead implies a formal investigation. In taking this position, we are resisting the act of colonisation by supporting a *relocation* that is about ongoing resources from their *located* place.

Continuing Bonds: the importance of re-membering

Continuing Bonds with the deceased was initially viewed as a symptom of pathological grief (Klass & Chow, 2011; Silverman & Klass, 1996). This model of grief dominated the mental health profession for nearly a century (Klass & Chow, 2011; Silverman & Klass, 1996). In this period, there was no distinction between types of bonds, functional or dysfunctional. There was also no distinction between those who prevented the bereaved from investing in new relationships and those who did not. With this perspective, a tie with the lost loved one was considered not to be beneficial to the bereaved. Any investment in this tie was misplaced. According to this model of grief, the presence of Continuing Bonds with the deceased represented the failure to 'move on' or 'let it go' so that the bereaved could invest in a new relationship (Klass & Chow, 2011; Silverman & Klass, 1996).

> 'My mother loved growing plants. She took pride in the garden, with its beautiful blooms, every summer. As an adult, I started to enjoy gardening and growing vegetables at my local allotment. This enabled my relationship with my mother to remain alive. Whenever I have beautiful blooms growing in pots over the patio, I feel my mother is present. This creates a sense of connection with her that is filled with love. I become a daughter again in that continued relationship.'
>
> (Samantha, co-author)

Bowlby (1980) described the death of an attachment figure as a prolonged process of protest, despair, and reorganisation as the survivor attempts to adapt to the loss. This process, at the time, required the patient to detach from the emotional investment linked to the bond with the deceased. This is considered to permit psychic and behavioural adaptation through investment in new relationships (Freud, 1957). In 'Mourning and Melancholia' Freud (1957) conceptualised his analysis of grief and mourning by defining love as the attachment (cathexis) of libidinal energy to the mental representation of the loved one (the object). According to Freud, when a loved person dies, their libidinal energy remains attached to their thoughts and memories. The psychological function of grief was for the individual to relinquish his bonds with the deceased and to regain his energy resources. According to his theory, an adaptive response to loss consisted of breaking bonds with the deceased to reinvest (or cathect) energy into creating new ties to living objects. The initial period of grief was spent mourning and then releasing the bond with the deceased.

'I grew up as a young woman in south Italy, and I observed that, when a loved one passed away, the spouse would continue mourning for the rest of their lives. In particular, if the bereaved was a woman, she would keep dressing in black.'

(Elisa, co-author)

Towards the end of the 20th century, there was a shift that opened the doors to new research into bereavement. This showed how the concept of Continuing Bonds is not only common; it can also be a healthy part of the bereavement process. In their publication 'Continuing Bonds: New Understandings of Grief,' Klass et al. (1996) made a major contribution to grief studies and reported that Continuing Bonds is a normative and healthy adaptation to bereavement. When describing what a bond is, Klass (2018) wrote: 'A bond is, in common parlance, love. Love is not a thing. It is not a feeling or emotional state within the self. Love is a relationship between two or more people. If we are to understand love, even love that seems pathological to us, we need to include all the parties in our observations.' Continuing Bonds is, therefore, about including all parties by reaffirming the presence of those who are no longer alive. This is part of the bereavement, as bonds with the deceased continue (Klass et al., 1996).

'I had a very close relationship with my grandmother, and, from when I was a young child, we used to watch the movie Sissi. We loved to talk about the historical characters and events connected to the movie. Now, whenever I miss my grandmother and the time we spent together, I watch this movie. I always leave a spot on the sofa next to me because I know she would not want to miss it.'

(Elisa, co-author)

When using Continuing Bonds in therapy, we are inviting in new stories. These are positioned as a form of resistance to dominant discourses about final goodbyes. Ultimately, this keeps the voice of past relationships alive and present (Rice, 2015; Hedtke, 2000; Hedtke, 2001; White, 1988). It brings in a new script, one that encourages a continual relationship where the client is not required to abandon their past identity. Instead, he is allowed to integrate the past with the present and possibly the future.

'As Yar waited for the inevitable refusal, his social worker suggested that he should receive a mental health assessment, and so it was that I supported him to see Ana. I'd expected to sit outside the room during the session, so I was surprised when he requested that I stay, and Ana agreed. Ana spoke gently to Yar and created, from his memory, a safe place he could visit when situations threatened to overwhelm him. As I sat in the room with my eyes closed, I could share the awakening noises of his home. His mother preparing the breakfast for the household, and the laughing chatter of his parents as they looked at their children eating at the table. His mother said, "My daughter looks just like me, but Yar is your son, and he looks just like you!" The bread on the table is warm, the honey is sweet, and the sun that is shining through the window is warm on their backs. A calm rested in that room we were in, our eyes brimming with tears. It was a privilege to witness that session, knowing that the slow process of healing was starting to take place.'

(Izzy, volunteer teacher and advocate)

In working with people who experience grief, 're-membering' also adopts a similar stance to that of Continuing Bonds, where the relationship with the deceased is brought back into the life of the bereaved (White, 1988). These re-membered stories give meaning, agency, and hope to the living (Hedtke & Winslade, 2004). In re-membering conversations, the therapist guides the client through the process with crafted questions. This builds a story of values and memories. The voice of possibility uses the verbs *could* and *would* to enquire into the areas of the relationship that the bereaved wishes to hold close (Myerhoff, 1982). Therefore, death can be seen not as a finality but as an invitation to a new relationship with the person who has died. Rather than generating stories of goodbye, therapy can seek to find ways in which the influence and values of the person who is no longer present can be brought into the life of the bereaved.

'In supervision, Rose described her own dislocation as she was pregnant and about to go on maternity leave. She talked about the fact that she currently needed to move houses and had her things packed. All the while, she and her partner and children lived with her own parents. She talked about a refugee mother called Damsa, who had become homeless with her small child. Rose was worried about ending her work with Damsa and the impact this might have on her. When Rose arrived to see Damsa, she noticed that she was wearing a scarf. It was an African scarf, not something that Damsa would normally wear. Rose complimented her on the scarf, saying how beautiful it was. Damsa told Rose she was wearing the scarf because, when she had been travelling by foot on her journey to the UK, she had lost sight of her child and was rushing around trying to locate her. Damsa talked about her fear and how frantic she had become. Then she described how, suddenly, she caught sight of her child. The child was wrapped in the very scarf she was currently wearing while being held by a stranger, an African woman. As Damsa approached and called her child's name, the woman passed over the sleeping child, wrapped in the scarf, which she signalled that Damsa could keep. While wearing the scarf that day, Damsa talked about remembering the kindness of strangers. The scarf reminded her of this and gave her hope.'

(Ana, co-author)

The idea of 'letting go' can also become a harmful story when grieving (Hedtke, 2000). This is because it does not allow for the past relationship to be a resource; rather, it becomes a rejection through the finality of loss. Furthermore, this creates a disconnection as it requires a move away from the identity the bereaved had with the deceased. In doing this, they may become someone different from the person they were in that relationship. This, in turn, can have an impact on the identity of the person bereaved. It can also impact how grief can be expressed in the present and in the future. We see this in people's responses to grief when they say, 'You just need to get over it and move on.'

Forgetting becomes an actual rejection of the present. This undermines and destructs the sense of the past and, in turn, the future. Forgetting entails a negation of time. On the other hand, when a person is encouraged to continue bonds with the deceased (Klass et al., 1996), they are given permission to remain connected to the influential voice of the deceased that has helped to shape and construct their identity (White, 2007). The person is allowed to have a past from which they can build their future and live in their present.

Continuing Bonds Enquiry: relocation as an action in the re-membering

Continuing Bonds Enquiry (Draper et al., 2022; Draper & Marcellino, 2023) recognises that identity is crafted by past relationships. These past relationships are then allowed in the present in order to support the creation of a preferred narrative. This form of *Continuing Bonds Enquiry* supports the connection to the existing resources in someone's story, bringing them back when they may feel lost (Draper et al., 2022).

> 'When I lost my mother, I was also expecting my second child. My griefheightened when my son was born. I realised that, in becoming a mother for the second time, I had reconnected to the loss of what I could not have in the present, namely the support, the wisdom, and the continued role of a grandmother to her new grandson. During that period, I felt static with this grief, unable to integrate this loss into my life. Only through exploring with someone who was able to witness for me was I able to recognise this.'
>
> (Samantha, co-author)

In our paper (Draper et al., 2022), we described the main themes of the *Continuing Bonds Enquiry* as being:

- **Identity:** who am I in the relationship(s)?
- **Hope:** what was, and what is, emerging for whom and from where?
- **Bonds:** the ties made from the relationship(s).
- **Time:** moving from the past into the present and the future.

The four themes are interconnected in the storytelling of the young people. By re-membering, we are allowing emerging identities to be named in the present. We are also bringing hopeful narratives that would otherwise have been left in the past with the loved one who is no longer present. In reconnecting with the bonds of that past relationship, the past identity returns to the present, where it can be integrated with the current one and can shape the future one. In this, there is a bridge between the past, via the present, to the future. What emerges then becomes a story about the past to tell in the future and share with future generations.

> 'My dad has always been present in my life, holding me to the next adventure of my journey. He was there when things were difficult. He was a dad, and, when needed, he was also a mum. He shifted and changed based on what I needed from him. After some significant losses in our family, I did not know how to say goodbye. He taught me that it was not about saying goodbye but about how we keep people's memories alive. He used to take me to the cemetery, where, every Sunday, we prayed together. It was like Mum, Grandma, and Auntie were there with us.'

> (Elisa, co-author)

As discussed earlier in this chapter, we will continue with a conversation we had with Hussain, which is as follows:

> 'My mum arranged for me to leave; my brother died, and she did not want the same thing for me.'

> (Hussain, young person)

This is an example of all four themes being represented in the story being told. Hussain talks about his 'identity' as a brother and son and the 'hope' in the arrangement to leave. It also situates the story in the past. The bond in the action of escape is facilitated by the relationship between mother and son.

The theme of 'hope' can be understood by the following example of a young person who was trafficked to the UK.

Table 5 Dialogical connections that are informed by the past in the present

Person speaking	What was said
Young person:	'Yes! I believe in beauty; they taught me to believe in beauty.'
Ana:	'Ah, so you are your name.'
Young person:	'I think so. I think they would want me to be respectful and kind.'
Ana:	'And the way you are – is that the beauty they intended?'
Young person:	'I don't know; I think they would want me to believe in beauty.'
Ana:	'What do you think your family would say about you now?'
Young person:	'That I am kind, and I respect people.'

In Table 5, the enquiry taking place sees me (Ana, co-author) ask about who named the young person. The young person states, 'They gave me a name that described what they believe about themselves.' I (Ana, co-author) reply by making a connection to 'her' name and 'their' beliefs. The connection is the word *beauty*. The young person is then able to own her belief and says, 'I believe in beauty; they taught me to believe in beauty.'

The theme of 'bonds' from our paper is reported in following paragraph:

- Hussain spoke about his desire to learn English and was asked, 'What would your mum say if she knew that you were learning English?' He responded that she would be very happy. He is reminded of the bond he has with his mother and how this will remain present whenever he speaks in English. That was her hope for him, and by bringing her hope to life, he is bringing her with him to the UK.

The theme of 'time,' as described in the same paper, can be understood by this example:

A young person was asked, 'What were you running away from?' He responded. 'From the army, as I did not want to become a soldier.' He was then asked, 'Who else in your family agreed with you?' This shows how his family, as an audience, is brought into the present where, otherwise, they would be absent. The action of agreeing for him to immigrate to the UK, which had been frozen in the past, was now alive and in the here and now.

A fuller example of a *Continuing Bond Enquiry* is described in Table 6. It is a dialogue between me (Ana, co-author), in my capacity as a therapist, and a young man, Firash. It uses the themes as a way of understanding what is being shaped and created. It is in relation to Firash, who has been refused asylum.

Table 6 Dislocation and the multiple faces of hope

Person speaking	What was said	Continuing Bonds Enquiry themes
Ana:	'It sounds like there is a high possibility that you will go back.'	Time: future possibilities
Firash:	'Yes.'	
Ana	'I see the fear, and yet I wonder what experience of being here you want to take with you?'	Identity: who he is in the present Bonds: the ties made with identity in the present
Firash:	'I don't understand.'	
Ana:	'Have you made friends? Have you learned anything?'	An expanding identity question
Firash:	'Yes, I have learned how to look after myself.'	Identity: I can look after myself. Bond: the learning that has taken place
Ana:	'Do you cook?'	Identity questions that increase the potential to thicken the description of who he is and what he can do

Person speaking	What was said	Continuing Bonds Enquiry themes
Firash:	'Yes, sometimes in the house, we share doing this.'	Time: sharing and present experience with possibilities in the future
Ana:	'You have learned how to negotiate who does what?'	Hope: in the new skills he has been able to gather and learn
Firash:	'We live together.'	Bonds: made from sharing a house together
Ana:	'Do you feel you have learned different things?'	Bonds: to the new learning that may have taken place
Firash:	'Some English, how to manage money, how to travel.'	Identity: as someone who is capable, and the bonds that have come from the learning that has taken place
Ana:	'These are amazing skills that many young people struggle to do, especially managing money.'	Hope: in the learned skills and his identity in relation to the bonds of speaking English, managing money, and navigating travel
Firash:	'I save my money so I can go to the mosque.'	Identity and bond: connecting in relationship to actions Time: in the saving, what I did in the past (save) allows me to go to the mosque in the present.
Ana:	'You save to be able to do what is important to you.'	A clarifying question about the hope that is emergent in his identity and bond
Firash:	'Yes, I want to go to the mosque; I have to go to London.'	He links the bonds he has already mentioned, bringing them together as a dynamic interaction. His bonds include saving money, travelling, and speaking English.
Ana:	'So, if you go back, you can take with you the ability to negotiate, to know what is important, and to get it for yourself.'	This statement brings together the different themes of identity, time, bonds, and hope.
Firash:	'Yes, but I don't want to go back.'	He connects to the themes and brings the present hope, in this moment in time, to remain in the UK.
Ana:	'Sometimes we can't change the decisions being made; sometimes we have to find ways beyond them. Can you take what you have learned, and the hopes you have realised here, with you?'	Here we start to introduce emergent hopes should he have to return to his place of origin, linked to co-author Ana's ideas about the multiple faces of hope (Draper, 2009).
Firash:	'Yes, but it is different there; I am scared.'	He links his identity to the asylum decision.
Ana:	'I can see that it is scary; what does fear make you do?'	An acknowledgement of his identity and a curiosity about time in the present and future

(Continued)

Table 6 (Continued)

Person speaking	What was said	Continuing Bonds Enquiry themes
Firash:	'It makes me want to run away, to hurt myself.'	He is able to link the identity created by the asylum decision to possible future actions.
Ana:	'You have made some difficult journeys – the one to get here, the one once you arrived, and all the learning you had to do. I wonder if fear is reminding you of how hard the previous two journeys have been?'	Time is key in this acknowledgement of his identity in relation to the past, present, and possible future.
Firash:	'Yes, I want to stay; I don't want to go back; I am scared.'	Here, he talks about his hope to remain in the context of an identity imbued with fear.
Ana:	'Did you feel fear in your previous journeys?'	Time is being explored in relation to past identity.
Firash:	'Yes, I was very afraid.'	Here, Firash connects to time as a cycle from which previous fear is present.
Ana:	'So, fear is stopping you from having hope? If you were able to negotiate with fear, to allow a little hope to be present, what would the hope be?'	In this question, Ana is linking to Firash in relation to his experience of fear and what it takes from him. She externalises fear to support Firash, to allow hope to be present in the moment in which the enquiry is taking place.
Firash:	'To stay here.'	Firash names a possible hope that is related to time. He links to the previous hopes imbued in journeys made to reach the UK.
Ana:	'And if you couldn't stay and had to go back, what hope could you have?'	Hope is further expanded now in its multiple faces. What other hopes might be possible in the present and future?
Ana:	'From when you left home and the learning you have done in the two journeys you have made, what of the learning will keep you safe and help you find your family? You said that you had learned that you can travel, you can save money to access important things, and you can negotiate with others.'	Hope and bonds are brought together in the enquiry. Time, as in the possible future, whatever happens with identity in relation to a decision made by the Home Office, the bond of what he has learned, the relationship with those he lives with, and his achievements are his to have and take.

Person speaking	What was said	Continuing Bonds Enquiry themes
Firash:	'Yes.'	He acknowledges the multiple faces of hope and the different time-oriented possibilities.
Ana:	'Will these skills help you in the hopes you have?'	A connection to his identity is made; in this, he becomes a hopeful person, a shift from the scared, fearful person.

This transcript demonstrates the flow of the themes embedded in the *Continuing Bonds Enquiry*. It shows that it is part of a flow within the relationship between the young man and therapist, and therefore the themes are not fixed to a certain moment in time. This example shows a coordination between the person enquiring and the person responding, in which they both manage and shape the meaning being made.

It links to a process of decolonisation by engaging in the rediscovery that supports a sense of recovery. It also allows for a sense of mourning over the potential loss of a certain life and future while supporting a new and emergent dreaming where different possibilities can take place.

Food as an act of re-membering: two supervision sessions

'Laura came to supervision and talked about her work with a trafficked child who was now in foster care. She spoke about using Continuing Bonds Enquiry in the nutritional work she was doing with him and his foster carer. Laura reported that she had a review with them both and came into their home to find the foster carer and young person speaking to his birth mother. His foster carer was keen to get his birth mother's recipe for his favourite food. They had been talking together about the food he loved, who had cooked it for him, and the memories associated with eating it. Laura reported that the foster carer and young person started to cook the recipe, given by his birth mother, together. By doing this, they could share in the ritual of eating and connecting to the location and relocation it shaped.'

(Ana, co-author)

'The social worker told me that Jennifer had been eating the same meal for dinner ever since she moved to a new accommodation. He then became curious about what this meal meant to her and where and with whom she was when she had it the first time. When Jennifer heard these questions, she smiled, sat straight, and said, "There were 10 of us at home. Mum did not have time to cook dinner, so she used to buy smiling face chips. That was our meal in the evening." I then asked the social worker what Jennifer was saying about herself through this story. He responded, "She is remembering her home and her family. She eats with them every evening. This is what is helping her cope.""

(Elisa, co-author)

Outsider Witness reflection notes you may want to make about Chapter 7:

- What 'sense' do I make of these Continuing Bonds Enquiry ideas in relation to my own experiences?
- What bond do I have with another person or a place?
- What smell, taste, sound, feeling, and temperature can I connect to a continuing bond?
- Who am I in this bond? How does this identity, with that bond, remain with me in my everyday life?
- How do I carry the bond? How do I share it, and with whom?
- How might these ideas change what I do in my practice?
- If I were to undertake a *Continuing Bonds Enquiry*, what would I need and who could support me to do this?
- What potential difference would such an enquiry make?

Chapter 8

Fast Feet Forward

Beyond arrival

'Your body hears everything your mind is saying.'

Author unknown

Since the first groups were run by the original Action Research team within Kent, we have gone on to develop and use the *Fast Feet Forward* way of working. By doing this, we have ensured that we continue to learn while delivering the *fast feet* work. We have, as part of the partnership work that has taken place, also captured the changes that have occurred for the children and young people participating. This has been one of the ways in which we have shared our evolving understanding of what has been taking place. These papers have been published, and we will reference them as we describe our findings.

'Seeing a group of young men doing fast feet work for the first time was awe-inspiring yet also terrifying. I knew I had to trust what they had told me. Their voices were central to what we were doing together. The coaches got the brief perfectly and were so relational in their approach to teaching the fast feet ladder work. The translators also started to participate and were in the flow of the process. Everyone's worlds collided, including a large sports shop in the town that provided trainers and sports clothes at a discount. We were all striving towards crafting something effective together.'

(Ana, co-author)

Fast Feet Forward was created with the intent to develop an intervention that could create resilience and support self-management, both in the present and future. This desire was driven by the distressing stories that the unaccompanied asylum seekers carried with them. We became aware of the need for an early intervention tool that could be delivered and how it needed to be different from the more traditional Westernised way of working that involves talking therapy.

'I asked Kevin, my partner, what ideas he had about how he simulates bilateral movement in sport, he being a triathlon coach. I wanted to know: could we

DOI: 10.4324/9781003258681-9

simulate the Eye Movement Desensitisation and Reprocessing protocols as an early intervention? Could we use this as a tool from which we could reduce the levels of disturbance being experienced in moments of dislocation? He came up with the idea of fast feet ladder work, and I tried it with a rope ladder in our back garden. It did exactly what I had hoped, and I was excited to think about its use with this group of children. That's how the Fast Feet Forward protocol was born. In trying the fast feet ladder myself, I saw that we could simulate Eye Movement Desensitisation and Reprocessing protocol. And in doing so, that young person could potentially benefit from learning to do this for themselves. I was really excited at the potential possibilities for reducing distress and supporting positive beliefs about themselves. My colleagues were brilliant at quelling my nerves as we brought young people together to participate. We ran the first group, and the young people reported that they were running beyond the group to manage their distress.'

(Ana, co-author)

Fast feet ladder work is a way of using bilateral movement to improve foot speed. To undertake fast feet activity, you start at one end of the ladder and move straight down it as fast as you can, being sure to touch both feet down in each square of the ladder, as a sequence of movement. There are different sequential ways in which the feet can touch the squares as a repeat and interactive activity in which left to right movement is undertaken. We go on to describe this further in the chapter.

In reviews, young people started to tell us about their use of the protocol. Here are several examples of what they told us:

'It felt really odd when I first started doing it, and it was hard to keep going because of everything that I was experiencing.'

(Naj, young person)

'I wasn't sure how this was going to help me.'

(Rekar, young person)

'I now do it every day while waiting for my appeal. It really helps me to manage the anxiety.'

(Issa, young person)

In the dislocation: finding new ways to run

The effect of complex trauma on a cohort of young people, where English was a second language while accessing talking therapy for most, was not the cultural or social norm in the countries they had left. We wanted to develop a protocol that was culturally and age sensitive, allowing us to acknowledge trauma in a non-pathologising way. What we heard from the young people was that telling their stories was difficult and could trigger distress in the retelling. Therefore, they would relive the trauma they had experienced. What seemed to be important was to develop a protocol that could act as an early intervention. This would integrate the minds and bodies of young people who were impacted by the multiple traumas experienced (Draper et al., 2020). It was also important to develop something that supported them in being resilient to the continual *dislocations* they might experience in the asylum seeker's journey.

Fast Feet Forward is a group protocol delivered twice a week, over a period of six weeks, for a total of 12 sessions (Draper et al., 2020, 2021, 2023). It combines Eye Movement Desensitisation and Reprocessing (EMDR; Shapiro, 1989; De Jongh et al., 2013) with the benefit of sports activities (Dolezal et al., 2017; Rodriguez-Ayllon et al., 2019; Dale et al., 2019). Instead of using the eye movement, as per the traditional Eye Movement Desensitisation and Reprocessing approach, *Fast Feet Forward* uses bilateral foot movements (Draper et al., 2020, 2021). This protocol differs from Eye Movement Desensitisation and Reprocessing in that it is an early intervention. It addresses trauma in the present rather than taking the past trauma event as a focus (Draper et al., 2020). The body, brain, and emotions were three critical components of the design of the protocol. Making links and connections to all three helped shape a holistic and more integrated intervention. This is referred to further on in the chapter (Figure 8.1).

'I loved Fast Feet Forward, although initially it did not make any sense as to why it should work. It felt weird to begin with, and I got tired and was really hot as the exercises we did were really fast.'

(Joseph, young person)

In the past few years, we have been collecting and analysing data about this protocol. This is so we can better understand its impact on young people's ability to process trauma and overcome some of their symptomatology. This protocol was used in our work with unaccompanied minors, adopted children, and looked-after children, with success both at a quantitative and qualitative level. We are embedding stories from multiple perspectives and experiences that link to and make sense of the statistical data that we have published.

The *Fast Feet Forward* protocol is divided into five phases (Draper et al., 2020, 2021). These are described in more detail further on in the chapter.

- **Phase 1:** names disturbance in the present (also called a hot spot, which is more fully described later on in this chapter).
- **Phase 2:** sees young people, supported by clinicians, identify the negative belief about the hot spot (e.g. I am dependent, I am unsafe). They then go on to produce a positive, preferred belief (e.g. I am independent, I am safe), always in relation to the hot spot.
- **Phase 3:** young people rate their Subjective Unit of Disturbance associated with the hot spot and the Validity of Cognition of their positive belief associated with the hot spot.

- **Phase 4:** coaches support young people to do the *fast feet* bilateral movements while young people hold their hot spot in mind.
- **Phase 5:** young people, once again, rate the Subjective Unit of Disturbance and their Validity of Cognition.

Eye Movement Desensitisation and Reprocessing addresses the past traumatic event once the person has reached safety in the present. In doing so, the safe place is enhanced to enable the person to access it with ease when needed. Some of the young people had safe place enhancements before the *Fast Feet Forward* protocol, starting as part of a *Continuing Bonds Enquiry*. However, during the actual *Fast Feet Forward* protocol, a safe place was not used unless needed. Some research indicates that trauma support should only be commenced when they are in a stable place (Sells, 2019; Allcock, 2019). Yet, for these children and young people, the reality is that life is full of uncertainty. Often, unaccompanied minors are in an ongoing state of distress from which a safe place cannot yet be envisioned. The trauma is ongoing and present in their everyday lives.

> 'I've got a letter from the Home Office with an appointment. I am so scared that I cannot sleep, eat, or think. I don't want to talk about what happened. It makes it all real again. I really don't want to go. It will bring it all back again.'
>
> (Najib, a participant)

Safety was developed in the relational context of the group. By creating a sense of togetherness, a community developed, from which there was a safe place for us all. It was evolving and changing, as well as responding to what was happening at the time and in any given moment. The intention behind this method was to create a relational web around the child, thus enabling them to feel safe and confident within the group setting.

> 'When Ahmed first arrived, I did feel scared of him. His anger was visceral, and you could see the other boys shrink from him. He was also easily activated and would square up to anyone who got in his way. His legs were scarred by what looked like old burns. Yet, slowly, he started to relax, to smile, and to engage, not only in the fast feet activity but in the relationships with the coaches and staff.'
>
> (Ana, co-author)

Phase 1: hot spots, the past dislocation through the present voice

A hot spot is a moment of disturbance in the present that becomes the targeted focus throughout the *Fast Feet Forward* session (Draper et al., 2020). The hot spot allows us to understand the impact of trauma on the everyday experience of a young person's life. We defined the work as dialogical because it creates a logical consciousness of the traumatic experience. This is in turn linked to the hot spot. The question asked is, 'What has distressed you in the past week?' (present event) rather than 'What are your stories of trauma?' (past event). The present event, such as 'losing a travel card,' is still linked to the past trauma of having travelled for months through Europe. We are not connecting the past trauma to relational life in the present (Shotter, 2015; Draper et al., 2021).

There are many hot spots that produce high levels of disturbance, which are linked to trauma. They are often not immediately obvious or easy to predict. In the first study (Draper et al., 2020), unaccompanied minors reported the main hot spots as sleeping issues. These included nightmares, missing family, worries about the future, being bored, not being able to attend school, not being able to go to church, and isolation. In the third study (Draper et al., 2023), the most common hot spot for unaccompanied minors was confirmed to be sleep difficulties.

'I couldn't believe it when Ana told me that one of the recurring hot spots is the lack of a bus pass. As a local authority, we have so many complaints from this group of children about not having access to a bus pass. And now that we are talking about it, it makes complete sense. I mean, these children have snuck onto lorries and other transport on their journey through Europe. Some also became injured, and some had hypothermia on arrival in the UK. Not having a legal means to transport makes them feel like they are still illegal and in danger.'

(Stella, social worker)

Fast Feet Forward research results indicate that the major hot spot for adopted children concerns difficulties at school. In understanding the hot spots themselves, we are able to think from a system-wide perspective about the *dislocations* that unaccompanied asylum-seeking children are experiencing in their everyday lives. We can then start to support these children to manage the hot spots that are a natural response to extraordinary events that have taken place in the past. This gives us an opportunity to be preventative and proactive in the care we give. It also supports us in finding ways to *relocate* these children.

When working with the interpreters for unaccompanied asylum-seeking children, it was problematic to explain what a hot spot was and how this could be translated. We realised that the interpreters were worried about influencing the young person's interpretation of the hot spot. After a few sessions, interpreters became clearer and more confident in communicating with young people and with us. They had a better understanding of the protocol and its application.

'I love being part of Fast Feet Forward. The first time I translated in the group was at the cricket ground in Canterbury. I felt part of the team and soon learned how to help the boys I was translating for. I helped them to make sense of what was being asked and to score their hot spots. I found myself running with the boys, encouraging them to do the ladder work, and cheering them on in their own language. Each session, I saw the difference we were making, the joy on their faces, and the weight of the world being lifted somehow.'

(Ruth, translator)

In addition, the young people were worried that they might say something that would jeopardise their application to stay in the UK. They were also really concerned about missing college, as this meant they would lose their bursary. Therefore, we had to ensure that the colleges were aware that this was a health appointment. They required reassurance from the interpreters that talking about their hot spot would not mean they would get into trouble for what they said. It felt important that these conversations were done confidentially, away from other group members, giving the young person privacy to say what they wanted. Sometimes this process could be quite lengthy. The interpreters enquired about the young person's week and the things they had done to help identify a hot spot with them.

'Blending fast feet ladder work with a trauma protocol started to make sense. The more I did it as a coach, the more I started to notice the difference it made. Physically, those participating would change. I don't mean from the exercise, but more from how they held themselves. Even the muscles in their faces seemed to relax and change shape. It's like they were uncoiling somehow.'

(Trish, coach)

Phases 2, 3, and 5: Subjective Unit of Disturbance and Validity of Cognition as outcome measures

The Subjective Units of Disturbance (Wolpe, 1990) are a measurement of the emotional impact of distressing memories. Young people were asked to evaluate their level of disturbance using an 11-point Likert scale, where 0 meant 'no disturbance at all' and 10 meant 'high disturbance.'

'I changed a bit. I was very engaged; there were some upset bits, and it became too tough for me. It can be tough and bring back memories, but there are therapists available for support. The school also saw differences in me after the Fast Feet Forward group.'

(Johnathon, young person)

Figure 8.1 shows an example of the Subjective Units of Disturbance scale. This uses a visual representation rather than just numbers. We developed the visual representation as a way of helping ease understanding as to what the measure means and its scaling.

The Validity of Cognition was developed by Shapiro (1989) and is a self-report measure. It is used to assess one's level of confidence and belief in positive cognition. It uses a 7-point Likert scale where 1 means 'not true' and 7 means 'completely true.' Figure 8.2 is an example of a visual representation of the scale that we created for the young people.

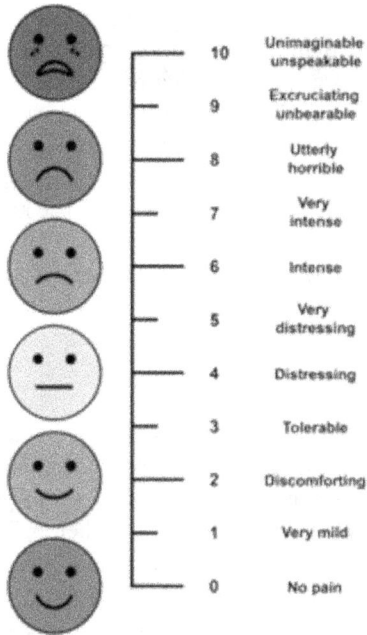

Figure 8.1 The Subjective Units of Disturbance scale adapted for young people.

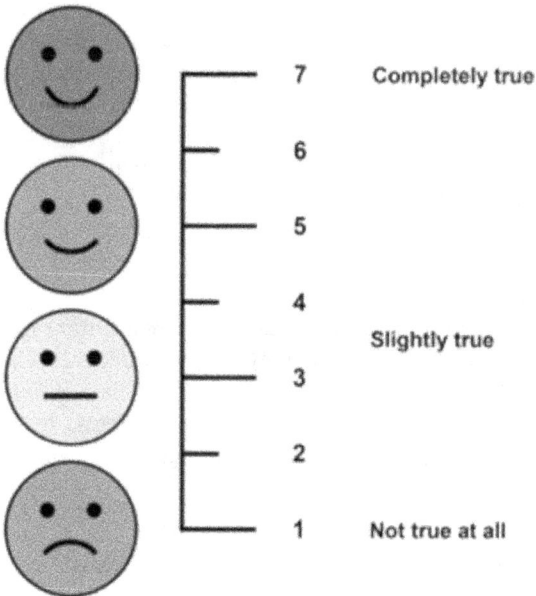

Figure 8.2 The Validity of Cognition scale adapted for young people.

The young people's beliefs in their positive cognition are connected to the trauma-related, negative cognitions being processed. Therefore, the Validity of Cognition is an indirect measure of trauma processing (Draper et al., 2020). An increase in these scores means that they believe more in their positive beliefs than the negative ones, which we will describe further.

> 'The young people thrived at Fast Feet Forward. The hardest part of the process was explaining the Subjective Unit of Distress and Validity of Cognition scores. However, this became easier as things went along. Also, when we got to know the interpreters better, they got a feel for what we were doing and were able to describe what was needed.'
>
> (Samantha, co-author)

Abdullah, a young person who attended the group, presented with a decrease in his Validity of Cognition as opposed to the more expected increase we had seen in other young people's scores. This may well be attributed to this young person processing some trauma event, which may then interfere with their belief in positive cognition.

The scales are interrelated yet separate. The Validity of Cognition scale is about the belief a young person has about an alternative way of understanding themselves. For example, the negative cognition related to a hot spot might be 'I am out of control,' and their preferred belief could be 'I am in control.' The scaling is about how true the 'I am in control' statement is compared to before they did the bi-lateral movements.

The Subjective Units of Disturbance are related to the level of emotional turmoil they experience when focusing on a hot spot, such as a bus pass that hasn't arrived, an interview with the Home Office, or being age-assessed. They name the hot spot that has been present since the last session and scale the level of disturbance they have experienced and continue to experience. At the end of the *fast feet* movement, they re-scale the disturbance level by re-connecting to the hot spot.

Both scales link in that the more positive a belief they have about themselves, such as 'I am in control,' the lower their level of disturbance is likely to become. Also, if their level of disturbance is lowered, they are more likely to have positive beliefs about themselves.

Some young people, such as Suliman, 24, chose to undertake *Fast Feet Forward* repeatedly. He continued to report high levels of disturbance as his asylum application was refused three times. His scores remained relatively unchanged, which would be indicative of his feelings of hopelessness. Yet he found the groups so helpful in the 'stuckness' of his situation that they contained him in the disturbance he was experiencing.

Phase 4: *Fast Feet Forward*: bilateral movements

In terms of the bilateral feet movements, we included: warm-ups, stretches, and lunges; *fast feet* ladder drills; run drills; high knees; high heels; the main set; shuttle runs; beep tests; Cooper's run; and cool downs (Draper et al., 2020). Kenneth Cooper, in 1968, developed a run test that suits all different levels of fitness and is challenging for everyone participating. The test includes running for 12 minutes to try to get as fast as you can. Embedded in the test is a cool down to reduce the likelihood of injury.

'I liked Fast Feet Forward because we did something proactive rather than sitting down.'

(Fazal, a young person)

The *fast feet* ladder work is made up of drills that shape the main activity and last about 30 minutes (Draper et al., 2020). These include one foot, two feet, one foot in and out, two feet in and out, lateral two feet, lateral one foot in and out, lateral two feet in and out, and a back pedal. As part of the protocol, clinicians also remind young people of their hot spot during the *Fast Feet Forward* work.

'When I did Fast Feet Forward, I found it very hard to start. This is because every time I tried to do an activity, I had flashbacks. Towards the end of the first two sessions, I started making friends. We all helped each other. We laughed and had fun doing it. It didn't matter that we were all at different ages. Fast Feet Forward helped me, and I still practise at home, which helps me feel better.'

(Kione, young person)

There was a lot of preparation in the process of setting up the group. We needed to consider time, location, and recruitment for the group. We also needed to help those who agreed to attend to understand the principles and structure that *Fast Feet Forward* would follow. We had to think about the self-care of the young people by ensuring drinks and snacks were provided.

The atomic model of *Fast Feet Forward*: the interconnection between brain, emotions, and body

The atomic model has been developed over time as part of a trajectory of knowledge from which the structure and composition of atoms were described (Draper et al., 2020). It supports an understanding of how things are made. This way of describing is, therefore, about inter-relational responses as a graphical representation. In this way, we can see positive changes that are concentrated in a small space at the centre of the nucleus. Pearce (1994), as part of the development of a practical theory called the Coordinated Management of Meaning, first introduced the idea that, in communication, we need to notice the importance of interactions. From here, perspectives, practices, and the effects of those perspectives and interactions can be brought together and understood.

'I felt like my brain had slowed down. I could feel myself feeling lots of things that I had never been able to describe before. It felt really weird, and I still don't understand how it works, yet I know I feel different.'

(Selassie, a young person)

We designed a version of an atomic model (Draper et al., 2020), inspired by Pearce (1994, 2004), for *Fast Feet Forward* as a way to visually demonstrate how it works and supports the processing of trauma in young people. There are three components of the atomic model that intersect with one another. These components are the brain, the emotions, and the body.

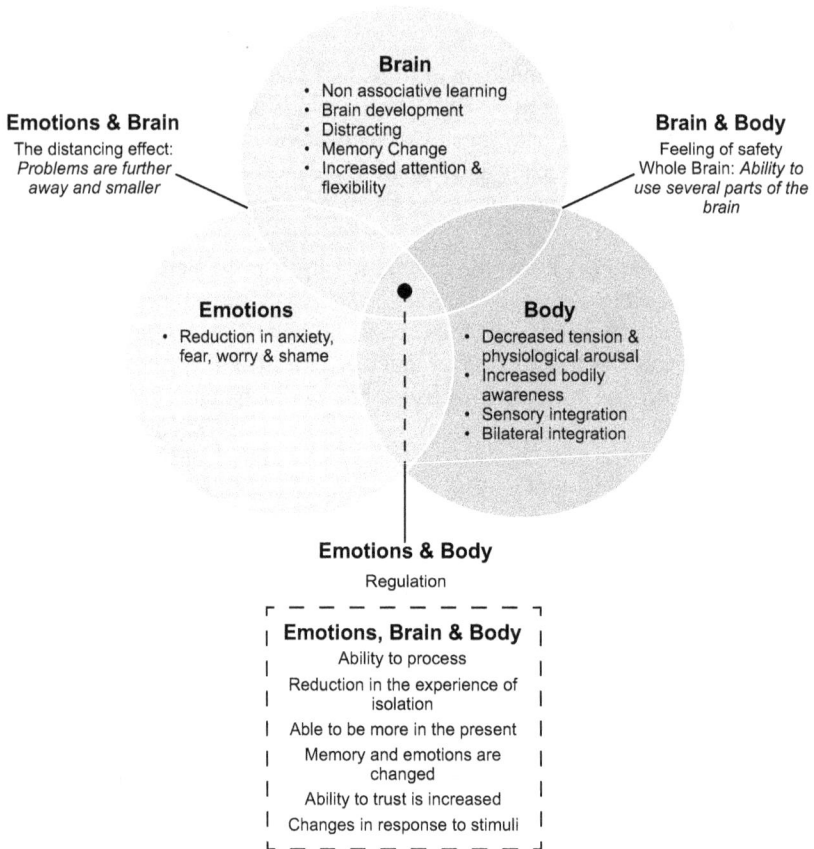

Brain
- Non associative learning
- Brain development
- Distracting
- Memory Change
- Increased attention & flexibility

Emotions & Brain
The distancing effect:
Problems are further away and smaller

Brain & Body
Feeling of safety
Whole Brain: *Ability to use several parts of the brain*

Emotions
- Reduction in anxiety, fear, worry & shame

Body
- Decreased tension & physiological arousal
- Increased bodily awareness
- Sensory integration
- Bilateral integration

Emotions & Body
Regulation

Emotions, Brain & Body
Ability to process
Reduction in the experience of isolation
Able to be more in the present
Memory and emotions are changed
Ability to trust is increased
Changes in response to stimuli

Figure 8.3 Illustrates the ways in which the Fast Feet Forward bilateral movements support a mind-body-emotion connection.

As previously discussed, our brains can change as a result of new experiences. This ability is called neuroplasticity. This can be enhanced rapidly through exercise (Basso & Suzuki, 2017). For instance, areas that benefit from exercise are the hippocampus and prefrontal cortex, as they are involved in memory and executive function (Duzel et al., 2016; Voss et al., 2013). The hippocampus was found to have the genesis of new neurons as a result of running (Basso & Suzuki, 2017; Cooper et al., 2017). Current research shows that exercise is beneficial to our brain function. It can also be a protective factor against developing neurodegenerative memory loss disorder (Duzel et al., 2016).

'I have met new friends from different countries. I am doing exercise with them, and it's nice to help each other. Everything is happy there. After I finish Fast Feet Forward, I go home, shower, and sleep. When I wake up in the morning, I feel happier; it is a good day. My brain works well, and I am thinking about my family in a good way.'

(Yosief, a young person)

Research has demonstrated that bilateral stimulation is associated with feeling relaxed and having more positive feelings (Amano & Toichi, 2016). Longstanding scientific evidence has already demonstrated the link between sport and the release of endorphins (e.g. Harber & Sutton, 1984). Bilateral stimulation has been investigated further in the past few decades, and the results are promising. We know now that bilateral stimulation increases activity in the superior temporal sulcus (area of memory representation). This indicates the connection between bilateral stimulation and the recall of representative pleasant memories (Amano & Toichi, 2016). Bilateral stimulation further reduces the vividness and emotionality of the traumatic memories (van den Hout et al., 2011; De Jongh et al., 2013; Engelhard et al., 2010b).

'I felt like I could think again; I could remember some good times for the first time in a long time.'

(Siddiq, a young person)

The young people, who had attended *Fast Feet Forward*, started using it at school and in their accommodation. Those who supported them started noticing the hot spot as they were able to name them. Once we are able to assign language to an experience, we are more capable of making sense of it. The support worker, teachers, and hostel staff began to encourage them to use the ladders to do *fast feet*. The feedback we received was that it worked. The young people were able to work through their hot spot (in the brain) through their body's bilateral movements.

As the brain changes, in response to a traumatic event, our body also 'keeps the score' (Van der Kolk, 1994) through a somatic memory of the event. Therefore, the *dislocated* body becomes part of the story of *dislocation*. A recent study highlighted the positive connection between sport and body image in a group of adolescents.

The parts as a whole: the system working together

As part of the planning to set up the group with unaccompanied minors, the use of interpreting services was essential to the process. Interpreters took part in the translation of the hot spot as well as the Subjective Unit of Disturbance and the Validity of Cognition at both the beginning and end of the protocol. This was in order to facilitate communication with young people. Also, they were invited, as part of the process, to participate in *Fast Feet Forward* through the use of ladders alongside young people and therapists.

> 'I love Fast Feet Forward; it is the best therapy these boys could have. And I love the fact that I am there with them, running alongside them and supporting them with the familiarity of their own language. They enjoy coming, and they love the fact that it feels so normal. They also tell me how much better they are feeling as time goes on. I think the fact that some are coming and will do their prayers, and that this is facilitated as part of the process, is fantastic. They (the children) don't want to miss it and find ways to manage things so they are able to come.'
>
> (Abrihet, Fast Feet Forward interpreter)

The two sports coaches, who were trained in ladder work prior to the group, led the entire sport protocol of *Fast Feet Forward*. This included the steps described in our paper (Draper et al., 2020), such as warm-up, ladder work, run drill, main set, and cool down.

One of the coaches wrote the following about participating in *Fast Feet Forward*:

> 'Along with the other coaches from the Weald Tri Club, I really enjoyed leading the Fast Feet Forward sessions. We've used speed ladders in our coaching for some time, and to find that they had a psychological impact as well as a physiological benefit was great. We enjoyed seeing the progression of the children and young people over the duration of the course. Though the work was often challenging in many ways, for those taking part, it was rewarding to see progress being made and young lives gradually transformed.'
>
> (Gary, Fast Feet Forward Coach)

Andy, a mental health nurse, describes being part of the development of the protocol in the following way:

> 'My memories of Fast Feet Forward are filled with fond admiration of the wonderful strength and resilience of the young people we were working with. They had been through such a struggle and were still able to get up and function in the alien culture and British complex etiquette they were immersed in.'

Teaching assistants, support workers, and residential workers were also invited to attend sessions to learn the protocol. They could also develop novel ways of managing complex trauma presentations outside of the group. They joined us while working alongside professional running coaches and interpreters. The young people reported finding this supportive. Having the presence of familiar adults gave a greater feeling of togetherness, enabling an integrated and *located* sense of self in the group.

> 'During a session, Rose did not want to participate. She was sitting in the corner of the sports hall, feeling anxious and uncertain about how to engage with the group activity of bilateral movements. One facilitator would just sit with Rose in these moments. By session three, another young person asked if she would accompany him in doing the ladder work together. Rose was able to engage with this support and joined in with the Fast Feet Forward process, having been encouraged by another member of the group.'
>
> (Samantha, co-author)

This protocol can be replicated in different contexts where there is an openness to work as a system, bringing together different professionals who all have different roles and participate together. Further description of the protocol in different contexts can be found in our papers (Draper et al., 2020, 2021, 2023).

The voice of a young person

We want to share a therapeutic conversation (Table 6) with Oman, which took place two months after the *Fast Feet Forward* protocol. At this time, he had turned 18, lost his social worker, and was told he needed to move from his accommodation. As well as this, his mother in Sudan was ill and needed surgery. He was also awaiting a court hearing, and his transport grant had not materialised, making it difficult for him to attend college. All major hot spots were being experienced in a short period of time.

Table 7 A conversation with a young person who attended the Fast Feet Forward protocol

Person speaking	What was said
Therapist:	'I can see that lots of difficult things have been happening.'
Oman:	'Yes, it's been difficult.'
Therapist:	'I'm wondering what has helped you to cope; you look different, like you are managing somehow?'
Oman:	'I did what you taught me.'
Therapist:	'What I taught you?'
Oman:	'Yes, you know, running.'
Therapist:	'So you ran?'
Oman:	'Yes, when I was sad or scared, I ran.'
Therapist:	'And what did that do?'
Oman:	'It made it better, it changed things, and it helped me cope.'

Oman was able to use the *Fast Feet Forward* protocol outside the group. He used this as a self-help activity, which reduced the disturbance levels he was experiencing. This helped him maintain his wellness despite the multiple *dislocations* taking place. He was able to *relocate* to positive cognitions about his own self-mastery. This enabled him to have agency and control. Additional support that maintained the unaccompanied minors' well-being came from a non-governmental organisation that was interested in the protocol. They got involved by contacting local cricket, running, and football clubs, enabling these children to join and continue to do sports together.

Fast Feet Forward: our voice as therapists

Further perspectives from facilitating *Fast Feet Forward* follow. These perspectives also show how young people moved from a place of *dislocation* to a place of *relocation* through their relationships with the interpreters, as per Abrihet's experience. The multiple relationships with those alongside them not only encouraged them to attend the group but also gave them the safety to bring *locating* identities into the group through the act of praying. This was facilitated by the interpreters as an active part of the relationship. The conversations enabled them to bring their own presence to the connections they made with the therapists, coaches, and young people. Facilitators were able to privilege these moments of connection with the young people's culture and faith, prioritising these aspects based on their own religious experiences. The sports hall became more like a place of safety, which allowed them to be who they are.

This is amplified by the following experience while participating in the *Fast Feet Forward* group:

'I was facilitating a group of 16- to 18-year-old male unaccompanied minors who had all arrived in the UK after crossing the English Channel. They had crossed in small boats or via the tunnel in lorries to gain entry into the UK. Coming to Fast Feet Forward created huge anxieties, as this was often associated with attending something that, in their experience, might mean retelling their trauma stories with the possible threat of further interrogation. As two white British-born women facilitating the group, the use of interpreters, who were from Afghanistan and Iran, was very important to us. This supported the young people to locate themselves in the group. Seeing someone who looked similar to them and spoke the same language helped them feel supported enough to relocate their sense of identity and take the risk of participating in the group. In addition to this, when they understood it was sports-based, this located them to become more accepting of the group. This was assisted by being given an invitation to pray during the break with the interpreters. The coaches were of mixed heritage and black British origins. This created an additional visual representation of difference. This enhanced the cohesion and appreciation of identity in the group. During the various tasks, there was a lot of laughter, cooperation, and appreciation for each other.'

(Samantha, co-author)

Here is Elisa's experience, as a psychologist, participating in the *Fast Feet Forward* group:

'The first time we ran Fast Feet Forward, I was nervous and unsure of what was expected of me. I had bought new trainers and leggings. I was thinking, "How am I going to manage this new setting?" As young people started arriving, I immediately realised that Fast Feet Forward was not a traditional therapy group. Something about the atmosphere turned the sports hall into a familiar place. As I said "hi" to everyone, I began to feel more relaxed, with a sense of location. In being together, it was still 'us,' yet we were bringing something new about ourselves. We were more informal, the dress code was different, and our bodies moved in the space with a different pace and agility. There were no space restrictions compared to the therapy room; there were no chairs to define how much space we needed; the entire sports hall was our space. As I noticed this, I started realising how the conversations we had were somehow different from the ones in the therapeutic room. The young people and I were sharing another identity, one that was needed at that time and place. I felt glad to be there and run alongside them just like a sister would do.'

Fast Feet Forward enhances a sense of agency for the different individuals who take part. These include therapists, interpreters, young people, and sports coaches. Everyone brings something about themselves that is valued and recognised by the others. This allows reciprocity and equality in the relationships and acknowledgement of the differences that everyone represents.

'We were running together, drill after drill, as she decided to hold my hand every session. Since day one, I have been there with her. She was running through her hot spots, and they were becoming minuscule compared to that moment. At that moment, she was not alone.'

(Elisa, co-author)

The transformation is not singular; it is not about being fixed. Rather, it is about 'being with,' about a mutual transformation in the process of learning together and a celebration of the multiple *relocations* taking place. One of the things we noticed was just how hard it was and the level of commitment that these young people exhibited. We were also aware from stories in the reception centre that they loved certificates of achievement as symbols of the hopes they had in coming to the UK. Certificates were duly collated for each young person, and we had a ceremony of achievement at the end of the six weeks as part of a celebration of what we had achieved.

• 'At the end of each group, we sat together on the floor, exhausted physically and mentally. We were also proud of ourselves; we were happy. Certificates of achievement were shared and read out to the group. As clinicians, we prepared the certificates together, and we noticed all the changes along with the difficulties and the achievements. It was the most beautiful moment, as a group, to be there and acknowledge what we had done together. We are always stronger as a community.'

(Elisa, co-author)

Outsider Witness reflection notes you may want to make about Chapter 8 are as follows:

- What 'sense' do I make of my body in response to the protocol being described?
- What hot spots do I have, and how do I manage them?
- How do I feel after physical activity – sore, relaxed, tired, hungry, thirsty, refreshed?
- How does this way of working link to sleep and nutrition?
- How will this change what I might, or might not, do next when working with trauma experiences in my practice?

Chapter 9

Curiosity gave the cat nine lives?

In this chapter, we will explore a way of being with unaccompanied asylum-seeking children that supports our understanding of the different contexts from which meaning and actions are derived. We should not work in silos but rather in a wider system in which each aspect has a part to play in meeting the needs of each child.

'No one can whistle a symphony. It takes a whole orchestra to play it.'

H. E. Luccock

We are all part of the journey these children make; their voices and ours are learning from and with each other. You, as an outside witness, are now also a voice with a story to tell, from which further learning can take place.

Maturana (1985) introduced the idea of domains, which are those of aesthetics, production, and explanation. This book, we would argue, is positioned in all the domains identified by Maturana, yet in this chapter we want to focus on the domain of aesthetics. We see this as a frame from which the other domains are activated and coordination takes place. This domain is set in a dialogical and story-informed position from which different perspectives are gathered and understood, with attention to power and ethics at the heart of our work.

The domain of explanation is about questions, questioning, and the exploration of different views and perspectives. It indicates a multiverse rather than one truth. Therefore, meanings are being made in the coordination taking place between people and the multiple ways in which the world can be viewed.

The domain of production is about establishing objective truth. There is, in this domain, a preferred way to see the world from which actions are taken and understood.

As humans, we are in relationships with each other and those we support. This means that we need to be conscious of the ethical dimension of our activities. Our relationship to each other has informed the implications of theory and practice, as well as the ethical position we take. Our ethics are linked to concepts such as hope, grace, ongoing bonds, resources, elegance, desire, and beauty. This is how the domain of aesthetics becomes the frame from which the domains of explanation and production flow. We ask questions that are about hope through the *Continuing*

DOI: 10.4324/9781003258681-10

Bonds Enquiry. We give sleep packs that are emotive in their smell, made up in a small box in vibrant colours, like a welcome gift.

In this work, we started from our clinical practice, where we linked this practice to theories that inform us and the ethics that we are mindful to maintain. The relationship is with us, as co-authors, and the children whose voices you have heard and are hearing. It is, therefore, in the domain of aesthetics (Lang et al., 1990) from which we engage and interact in our *Location, Dislocation, and Relocation.*

An example of this in practice is when a child is required to undertake an age assessment. Often, the challenge lies in determining their age. In a local secondary school, it is easier to see the difference in physical development of children at the same age. We only truly know their age because they have the paperwork and a healthcare system that verifies it. There is further complexity in defining an age for unaccompanied children because of the arduous journey they have made and the accelerated ageing that takes place in their bodies because of this. There are also multiple perspectives on ageing that come from cultural and ethnic differences. There is also the need to ensure the safety of a potential adult attending a local school as a pupil. Within the dilemmas faced by social workers, we should think about the child who is being age assessed and other children in the local community who need to be safeguarded. It is by holding these dilemmas with them that we were able to hold a more complex position, with varying dilemmas, from which we responded.

We need to think about global law and the context in which we work to elaborate, maintain, and/or support the move towards diverse viewpoints. It is helpful to have a guiding principle from which we can measure, question, and engage in diverse narratives. The global law, our guiding ethical principle, is Article 22 of the United Nations Convention on the Rights of the Child (1999). This article asserts that unaccompanied asylum-seeking children should:

- Receive the appropriate protection and humanitarian assistance in the asylum process.
- Be treated with humanity and respect.
- Have their voices heard.
- Have the best interest of the child principle applied to them when decisions are made about their future.

It is within the spirit of global law that we have sought to co-create multiple ways of viewing the lived stories in action. This has helped us to draw on the stories lived and told, as well as being curious about untold, unknown, and undigested stories in the hide-and-seek of being an unaccompanied child (Pearce & Pearce, 1990; Johnston & Robinson, 2017).

Bringing the learning together

This book presents a newly developed, social constructionist and narrative framework of therapeutic tools that can be used to support unaccompanied asylum-seeking children. We began to use the three different domains to think about our learning (Lang et al., 1990).

Having grown from an Action Research project, we started in the domain of explanation. In the process of reflecting on the explanations emerging, we developed clear and agreed goals linked to system-wide aspirations. These went on to develop into a work plan in the domain of production. The aim was to promote strong cross-professional relationships and inter-agency discussions. Using a dialogic methodology helped us reflect on the need to provide an intensity of support at the point of crisis, for example, when unaccompanied asylum-seeking children arrive in the host country and begin the process of applying for asylum.

The Action Research project aims were articulated by the following aspirations:

- All unaccompanied asylum-seeking children in reception centres with compromised emotional health and well-being are identified.
- All unaccompanied asylum-seeking children in reception centres are offered screening using a validated and culturally appropriate tool with respect to their emotional health and well-being.
- All unaccompanied asylum-seeking children in reception centres have an identified emotional health and well-being multi-disciplinary team meeting using a dialogical framework from which care is delivered.
- Measured improvements are seen in unaccompanied asylum-seeking children's emotional health and well-being.
- There is an increased ability and confidence of staff to provide interventions with respect to identified emotional health and well-being requirements.

This work took place using a network approach in which social workers from the local authority, educationalists, non-government organisations, spiritual leaders, and the National Health Service met and worked together to agree on and deliver these aims. Ultimately, by working together towards a nurturing system, we were creating better chances for these children by supporting and reducing the impact of their isolation and presenting needs.

The *Location, Dislocation, and Relocation* framework can be used as guidance for a multi-agency and multi-professional template of care delivery. It recognises that there are many agencies and professionals working with unaccompanied asylum-seeking children who provide psychological support and interventions. Every contact and interaction with a young person can enhance their resilience and improve their mental health and well-being. A close network of relationships between professionals aimed to reduce the sense of isolation in the children by creating the possibility of a nurturing system around them. Justice for these children is a slow coming together, a series of cycles, interactions, and coordinations with the child at the centre.

The World Health Organisation (2019) describes three different levels from which to organise thinking about healthcare systems. Those levels are the Macro, Meso and Micro. They are separate and yet interlinked, with each driving the other

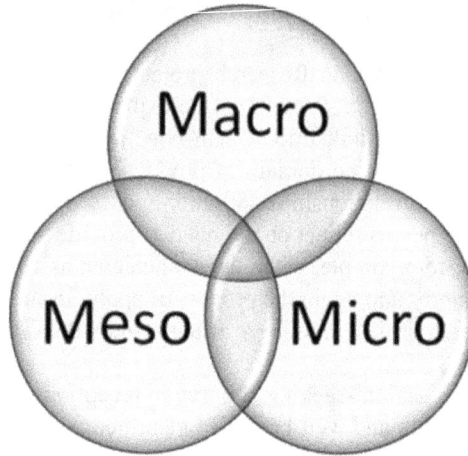

Figure 9.1 Macro, Meso, and Micro interlinked.

so that services are delivered and change can happen. This description can be linked to Cronen and Pearce's communication model, the Coordinated Management of Meaning, in which they describe all meaning as context-dependent (Jensen & Penman, 2018). As in Chapter 8, we are using a graphical representation to show how we developed our thinking. At the centre of the nucleus is the intensity of support at all levels to ensure that needs are identified and met during *dislocations*. The nucleus is a culmination of the stories we have gathered and the understanding we are gaining from the links we are making (Pearce, 1994).

The Macro level is society as a whole, for example, political, economic, and social factors. At this level, we are focused on the political narrative, economic contact, and social factors. These link to how a young person experiences those around them, how they are supported around their asylum claim, and how they are hosted.

In 2015, David Cameron, the then British Prime Minister, gave an interview to the British Broadcasting Corporation about the 'Calais Jungle,' where asylum seekers gathered to make a crossing to the UK. In that interview, he stated that a 'swarm of migrants (were) crossing the Mediterranean.' The Refugee Council, which works with refugees in the UK, said his comments were 'irresponsible' and 'dehumanising' (UK Politics, 2015). The British government continues to employ such rhetoric. Recently, in 2022, during a debate, the UK Home Secretary defined migration as an 'invasion.'

The Meso level is made up of parts of society that are organised into groups or organisations that look at technical and ethical delivery. In response to the Macro level, the political, economic, and social needs of these children have resulted in a lack of care and safety.

'In a careful judgement handed down today, Mr. Justice Chamberlain held that Kent County Council was and is acting unlawfully in refusing to accommodate and look after unaccompanied asylum-seeking children in their area when notified of their arrival from the Home Office. Instead, these vulnerable children have been and continue to be housed unlawfully in hotels by the Home Office, which are unsuitable for them, and where they are denied protection and care from a local authority corporate parent.'

(Doughty Street Chambers, 2023)

The same judge described these children as having the following:

'Been lost and endangered here, in the United Kingdom. They are not children in care who have run away. They are children who, because of how they came to be here, never entered the care system in the first place and so were never looked after.'

(Doughty Street Chambers, 2023)

The argument becomes about technicalities and ethics. Are these children in the care system or not? Whose responsibility is it to look after them and be responsible for the judgements being made about the lawful need for a corporate parent? The Macro and Meso are therefore linked together at these different levels in that the power is discursively distributed between what has come to be termed in the United Kingdom as a 'hostile environment' for asylum seekers. In 2012, the then Home Secretary, Theresa May, introduced a set of policies with the aim of making life difficult in the UK for those who could not show the right paperwork.

She said the following at the time:

'The aim is to create, here in Britain, a really hostile environment for illegal immigrants.'

This 'hostile environment' remains, and the experience of children in response to it is also affected. They have become a swarm of dehumanised and vilified pests that need to be controlled. The Micro level is the action of the individual and the wider intention from which the Meso and Macro connect.

'It was a racist attack on him, unprompted and out of the blue. It has really set him back. He is using the night light; it's like he is back at the very beginning again.'

(Precious, non-government organisation worker)

This young person, in the experience and act of being attacked, collided with the Macro and Meso. When there is a political discourse about hostility, that hostility is acted out with the 'other' being a target. Again, power is both discursive and material at all levels.

How should we, therefore, respond to the young person being attacked? How do we support them to externalise those experiences of racism as being something other than about them, although they have experienced it as a personal attack?

From the domain of aesthetics, here are some pertinent questions we should be asking:

- How can we become concerned with the experience, knowledge, and action of being excluded and marginalised?
- How do we explore these structures of oppression and the impact of living in a hotel and/or experiencing violence?
- How do we hear and amplify the voices of those who are affected by these kinds of oppressions?

When we look at the different levels, we see that each is operating at the same time, yet they are linked and interinfluence. From the previous descriptions given at the different levels, we see that what is happening at the Macro has an impact on the Meso and Micro. And what is happening in the Micro has an impact on what is happening in the Macro and Meso.

At the Micro level, children have been placed in hostels, which contravenes their human rights. It is then that the Macro comes into play, with organisations (such as a legal chamber) that take the Micro experience and challenge the way power is used, which is embedded in a 'hostile environment.'

At times, we have written reports for lawyers representing young people whose asylum claim has been rejected. It is in the domain of explanation and production that we join others at the Meso and Micro levels to ensure that the experience goes beyond a therapeutic approach to trauma. Yet it is a response to society in which we use ideas of social justice, empowerment, and critical consciousness. This links the personal journeys of those affected, from which we can participate in the recovery of collective memory so that justice can take place (Comas-Díaz & Torres-Rivera, 2020).

Liberation psychology (Martin-Baró, 1994) connects the individual journeys of those who socially struggle as a collective memory recovery process and ethical social transformation. These ideas connect to Chapter 7, where we discuss colonisation and the need to consider how we can form acts of resistance. These acts of resistance can ensure that our enquiry is about rediscovery, mourning, dreaming, commitment, and action. Each of these is linked to the steps of decolonisation that need to continue to take place (Laenui, 2000).

Attention to the connections between the Macro, Meso, and Micro levels has inspired us in the implementation of the *Location, Dislocation, and Relocation* framework. We have interacted at all these different levels, and this continues to be an evolving process from which we can learn and adapt our work. When we work in isolation, there is still a need to ensure there is accountability and responsibility for our work. It is by holding in partnership that we can meet the emotional health and well-being of these vulnerable children.

There is a clear need to build bridges between services and vulnerable young people. By interlinking the Macro, Meso, and Micro systems, we enable the possibility of early intervention. Furthermore, we could increase sensitivity and the ability to coordinate and strengthen accessibility for additional support, if required.

This way of working is embedded in the belief that children's emotional health and well-being are everyone's business. The *relocation* tools are based on the needs of the young person and can be used by a range of professional groups, including social workers, psychologists, psychotherapists, counsellors, psychiatrists, nurses, general practitioners (family doctors), border agency staff, police officers, children's solicitors, and others who are eligible to work with these young people. Our clinical experience suggests that this way of working could enable more positive interactions among professionals and better outcomes for young people. There is also a need for a consistent approach that supports a more holistic understanding that makes sense of the body/mind connections. There is a need to enable all involved and engaged in the care of these children to have tools from which they can enhance *relocations* from a resource-based position, yet also be mindful of the whole person from whom links and connections can be made and needs met.

Sharing the *relocation* tools with professionals supports us in engaging and connecting with our own lived experience and how this impacts what we see and do. This enhances our capacity to reflect on our work with young people. We have also learned how useful others have found this way of connecting in their ability to gain new ways of seeing and being in their own personal relationships.

'The workshops have allowed me to look at both my bonds with patients and my internal processes in a new way. I have found myself using the new vocabulary a lot to describe and relate to people in my life.'

(Mateusz, psychiatrist)

Thus, it goes beyond merely being a professional; rather, it enables us to be fully present and human in moments of dialogue and connection. It is a dialogical process of exploration, curiosity, and meaning-making.

Like Alex, the young person we spoke about in the introduction to this book, there have been steps towards understanding in the multiple dialogues that have taken place. Therefore, the *Location, Dislocation, and Relocation* framework contains all the voices of those who have contributed to deepening the learning taking place. The children and young people, social workers, support workers, nurses, doctors, foster carers, managers, directors, and commissioners have all contributed.

How is evidence captured?

With curiosity engendered in the context of asylum-seeking children, we need to keep in mind the differences associated with age, culture, ethnicity, religion, bodily responses, and other factors from which we understand how to respond.

Researchers who work with people who experience migration, which includes asylum seekers (Bhugra, 2020), should consider the following:

- The research should be culturally appropriate.
- It should be inclusive of minorities.
- It should have appropriate, equitable funding.
- It should have culturally informed hypotheses.
- It should involve a mix of qualitative and quantitative methods.

During our journey, these points became apparent in the course of our interactions
with children and young people in the way we hear the stories being told and make
sense of how we go on together. As those outside academia, we often think evidence is something that someone else gives us. It is as if we are looking to others
as the experts, from which we devise what we do and how we do it. Yet, all communication is data, and as humans, we are processing data all of the time. It is in
the process of making sense of what is being communicated at the different levels
that we can engage with what the different types of data are telling us and what we
go on to do.

In the Action Research project, when we started to hear the stories about sleep,
we noticed how some children were nocturnal (awake at night and asleep in the
day). This was in response to the journey through Europe that they had made. We
started thinking about our own experience with jet lag and the impact that had on
us. In making this connection to ourselves and our own lived experience, we were
able to 'thicken' the stories known and told about sleep (White & Epston, 1990).

We then began to 'produce' the evidence that came from who we are with each
other (Pearce, 2006) and started to make the connection that not all of their sleep
difficulties were a trauma response. In this way, we are in the flow embedded within
the different domains. We are in the domain of explanation, from which the story
became thickened. We move into the domain of production, from which we start to
think about what the needs are and what our response should be. In the movement
between these domains, we are being held within the domain of aesthetics. The
sleep packs became something we produced with the young people, who then went
on to share their knowledge and gift them to each other. In doing this, we were also
purposeful in supporting them and those connected to them to enable their sleep
needs to be identified and met.

The sleep packs were a whole system response. In developing them with young
people, we had to ask for help from businesses and the local community in the sup-
ply of the items required. In response to the stories about sleep we shared, we had
offers of help. One offer was that the King Singers, a famous acapella group that
performs around the world, host a concert in a village close to one of the reception centres. They donated all of the proceeds from that one concert to buy sleep
packs for this group of young people. Since then, the Separated Child Foundation,
a charity based in the UK, has supplied sleep packs for all unaccompanied asylum-
seeking children arriving in the country, on request from local authorities.

This led us to think that, as professionals, we could be more curious and 'refracted.' It is only then that we become aware and can use the multiple lenses through which new understanding and knowledge emerge. For us, the term *refracted* has come to mean a way to adapt the knowledge that we can see and adjust from different perspectives and perceptions to capture different types of knowing. This links to ideas within cybernetic theory (Bateson, 1967), in which we look to scaffold performance in both single and multiple phases of application to the action of being a professional. As professionals, we are the ones who often gather data that is informed through the privilege of being in conversation, and we need to share the findings to inform others so that they too can participate through a shared understanding.

During a presentation, we started to develop and play with the idea that in our refracted practice, applying curiosity is professional rigour. The following questions are examples that can help us shape the positions we take as those walking alongside these children:

- What stops me from being curious and noticing?
- What helps me to notice and reflect on my learning?
- When am I best placed to be in the action of knowing?
- When and how would I know who else needs to hear and understand?

For us, the first step was the new understanding that emerged out of the Action Research methodology (Ponte & Smit, 2007). Its focus is on the voices and stories told by unaccompanied asylum-seeking children. It draws on the experience of clinicians and the clinical reflections of the use of this framework within the agencies we have worked with.

This includes local authorities, charities, and the National Health Service. Each partnership has provided us with new learning and a new way of using this framework, which has resulted in facilitating presentations, writing papers, and writing this book. It is less about what we do to young people and more about what we do with them, with each other, and how we are together. This, we believe, is the difference that makes the difference (Bateson, 1972). This underpins the *Location, Dislocation, and Relocation* framework (Chapter 2), where, in our curiosity, we remain orientated to the stories being told and how we find solutions together.

When we started the Action Research project in Kent, the literature did not identify many early intervention protocols to prevent chronic mental health in this cohort. We, therefore, only reviewed the existing clinical ideas to support the development of this new framework once we had become immersed in children's stories. In doing this, the different ideas created and shaped what we did next.

The *Location, Dislocation, and Relocation* framework is gaining an evidence base through both qualitative and quantitative methods. Qualitative evidence includes the varied feedback received from clinicians and young people. Quantitative evidence includes the analysis of a range of data collected over the past years (Morgan, 2018).

This, therefore, links to our reporting and engaging as 'refracted,' in that we see different things at different times. In articulating what we see through different modes of communication, we are building an evidence base in the domain of production, which is framed by the domain of aesthetics (Lang et al., 1990).

The first set of data we collected was from the *Fast Feet Forward* groups. The process of developing this protocol came from the stories we were told about what was needed and would make a difference. As a response to the conversations we were having, the needs that were present, and our understanding of other ways of working, we explored ways in which we could take our practice forward.

The protocol was refined each time we ran it. The measures were redrawn to support understanding, and the questions asked were simplified to enable articulation. And so it progresses, and we hope to see it continue to evolve as a relational tool. In being relational, it looks to enable children to have a way of enhancing their emotional health and well-being in crisis moments and during transitions.

> 'For me, it is very important just the way you see a patient/person, not based on his/her trauma but on his/her resources. That there is always a 'good place' where you can relocate that person based on resources. Very inspiring is this kind of 'sensual' (based on senses) way of looking at people's experiences.'
>
> (Anna, psychiatrist from Poland)

The benefit of implementing and continuing research has enabled us to understand the potential for replicability. We are also continuing to articulate what it is that we are discovering. More recently, we have collaborated with a group of colleagues in Poland and supported them in their work with Ukraine refugees. Separately, we have also introduced this way of working with Ukrainian refugees who have found safety in the UK in 2022.

In using the *Location, Dislocation, and Relocation* framework in these different contexts, in addition to working with unaccompanied asylum-seeking children, we have discovered how this can be applied. Yet, there is so much more to discover.

> 'I'm not sure that young people understand the validity of cognition and the self-reported levels of disturbance. I think we need to measure it differently; have you got any ideas?'
>
> (Katie, psychologist)

In Chapter 8, we presented the smiley face measures we developed as a result of these types of conversations. They were in response to what the translators and children were saying about their ability to understand the scales we were using. The measure has also been translated so that children and young people who can read have access to the measure in their own language.

اداة فحص الضائقة

لماذا أنا ....؟

استخدامها

يرجى وضع دائرة حول الرقم (0-10)
الذي يصف أفضل كم محنة كنت تعاني في الأسبوع الماضي بما في ذلك هذا اليوم

قائمة المشاكل:
أشر إلى ما إذا كان أي مما يلي يمثل مشكلة لك في الأسبوع الماضي

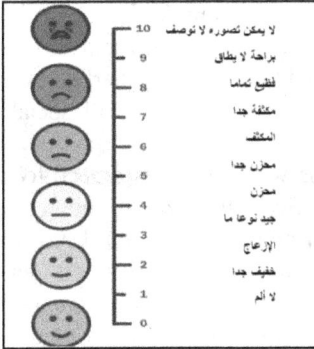

10 — لا يمكن تصوره لا توصف
9 — براحة لا يطاق
8 — فظيع تماما
7 — مكثفة جدا
6 — المكثف
5 — محزن جدا
4 — محزن
— جيد نوعا ما
3 — الازعاج
2 — خفيف جدا
1 — لا ألم
0

روحي:
فقدان أمل
فقدان الممارسة الروحية
فقدان المجتمع الروحي
غير راض عن كيف تعيش الحياة
فقدان السلام

عائلة:
التنقل
فقدان الاتصال مع العائلة
قلق بشأن سلامه الأسرة

جسدي:
إعباء
الإمساك
نوم
الهضم

عاطفيا:
خوف
القلق
الكوابيس
الكأبة

أخرى: ....
....

Figure 9.2 The Distress Screening Tool translated for young people.

In doing this, we not only responded to the facilitators' dilemma but also thought about the *relocation* that could be formed by seeing and being able to read your language of origin.

The journey can be rocky

In this section, we want to share some of the difficulties we have encountered in the work we have done. We are focusing on the *relocating* tools such as *Sleep Work, Distress Screening Tool, Semi-Starvation,* and *Fast Feet Forward.* Yet, these are not the only difficulties we have encountered. In sharing this aspect of the journey we are making, we are giving an account of what works and doesn't, from which we can try to find ways forward together.

Despite some positive outcomes, there have been some limitations to our work and the data collected. For example, due to the ever-changing circumstances (e.g. multiple changes of social workers, being moved on the National Transfer Scheme, changes in housing and schooling), it was not possible to predict the long-term effects and efficiency of some *relocation* tools, especially *Fast Feet Forward.* Therefore, inferences cannot be made about the durability of this protocol.

An area that created some difficulty was the understanding of the sleep tool. In the multiple transitions being made and in critical moments, there would often be a re-occurrence of a disordered sleep pattern. The culture of support services is often a tick box, in which the *Sleep Work* is seen as being completed. Yet like every human being we know, sleep is not a static behaviour but rather dynamic; it is activated into a different pattern in response to what is taking place. Therefore, in moments of *dislocation*, there is a need to review and support the young person to manage the disordered sleep patterns taking place.

> 'Sleep is in the water – it's like we just get it better and they are moved, or something awful happens and we start again. The sleep packs are great in that they can start to use the night lights again, yet a new bed, a new room, or a new environment all dislocate them. Sometimes it's like we have to start all over again.'
>
> (Gill, social worker)

Sleep Work is a recursive relational process where there is a need to check in and manage presenting needs. The *Distress Screening Tool* is another aspect of the framework that requires a relational, responsive approach. Like sleep, distress is heightened according to what the child or young person is experiencing. Therefore, like *Sleep Work*, in times of transition and in critical moments, there is a need to be mindful of the rising levels of distress. This is coupled with supporting a shared decision-making process through the solution-focused aspect of the tool. This type of support enables the young person to experience a sense of agency, therefore reducing the need to strive for it through negative behaviours.

Another challenge was highlighted in a supervision session during which the supervisee described the attempts to support the building up of a network around a young person. This aimed to address the young person's needs from a physiological perspective and their connection to the *Semi-Starvation Work*.

Table 8 A transcript of a supervision session

Person speaking	What was said
Melody:	'He has started to run away; he has gone missing, and everyone is worried about the level of risk. He is being moved to a foster placement, and he really doesn't want to go; it's yet another move, and he has lost all control.'
Ana:	'So, the control for him is in the risk; his needs are met when the risk is high. Yet he also loses control in that others make decisions about him.'
Melody:	'It's like a catch 22, and things are just getting more and more risky.'
Ana:	'Can you help him to have some control? Can you help him find the controls he does have? Can the network support him to gain control in a way that is not about running away?'
Melody:	'You're talking about distress screening and helping us to give him control? I'm not sure when we did that last; it's something we need to do again.'

'I kept saying, have we looked at their sleep? Have we looked at the constipation? Is there overflow? What are their sensory needs? How is their behaviour linked to a loss of control? They keep leaking faeces, and we are saying this has to do with their mental health, yet has their family doctor looked at the possibility that they might be impacted?'

(Ana, co-author)

This is central to the framework, as the aim is to enable professionals to challenge the body/mind split and to be curious about different possible stories from which new meaning can emerge. A silo way of thinking and a preference for 'single' narratives still remain prevalent in the social care and mental health systems we work in.

In Chapter 6, we have discussed the body/mind connection and the need to be mindful of both at the same time. Yet we often deny a person's needs because the needs don't fit with our 'help' expectations. For example, a child can be refused support because they are considered too risky, yet they can also be refused support because they are not risky enough. Therefore, the child becomes someone else's problem. This type of process is a double bind. Double binds are communication dilemmas that arise from a conflict between two or more messages. The conflict created is reductive and madness-making, which in turn makes for a sense of stagnation and/or chaos (Bateson et al., 1956). This way of working shapes a systemic failure where the most vulnerable are compromised, which can be madness-inducing.

We experienced this with regards to the *Fast Feet Forward* protocol in the different dilemmas we faced whilst delivering the group in the past years. One of them was attendance, which has been problematic. There were key issues that needed to be addressed, and it was difficult to manage them. The young people's bursary was linked to college attendance. Colleges would often penalise the young person by deducting from the bursary due to the fact they had attended the group, which meant they missed a session at college. There was confusion and a lack of clarity as to whether the group had a health appointment. This meant that it was not seen as important to support the young person to attend, and a mixed message was given about attendance. Despite many attempts to resolve these issues, they remain a barrier.

Factors that created huge *dislocations* for the young people included being in the UK for a short time, sometimes only days, when a referral was made to the National Transfer Scheme, which involves people moving to a different location in England. Other young people were also reported 'missing,' with links to trafficking and debt bonds. Children, young people, and their families can be manipulated and tricked into using human traffickers to give 'free' passage to another country. Yet the reality is that there is a debt owed to the trafficker for free passage, where the young person is forced to labour with little or no pay to repay the debt (United Nations Human Rights, 2023). On arrival in the

UK, young people are contacted by their traffickers to commence the work that will repay the debt of travel. This is modern-day slavery, with children reporting being physically 'branded' as belonging to the gang of traffickers, with no way to escape or to pay the debt.

> 'I didn't know what was happening. I felt overwhelmed and exhausted. I didn't understand what I needed to do. I wanted to do the right thing, yet nothing made sense to me.'
>
> (Safi, young person)

All of the above requires a whole system approach from which the safety of the child is maintained. It is also about supporting essential and coherent understanding within any therapeutic group, with key information about a young person shared. In response to these difficulties, facilitators prioritised information gathering. Yet, this quickly became a singular task rather than a partnership with referring agencies. Every partner's knowledge is key to shaping a dual understanding of the young person. In a spirit of partnership between the referring agency/clinician, the young person, and the group facilitators, decisions in context could have then been made. Those decisions could have supported access to the group while also supporting the time that intervention could have been the most beneficial for the young person.

We found that it was essential that the young people who attended were accompanied to the sessions by a known key worker. This was usually the residential support worker and, on occasion, the young person's social worker. Again, without this relational support, the young people found it difficult to continue to attend. In part, they struggled to maintain routine, often having newly arrived in the UK or having experienced further changes to their environment. Also, at times they were still struggling with sleep patterns, so they were asleep during the day when the sessions occurred.

The referral list of young people was significantly larger than the participant group and changed on a weekly basis. Greater rigour was sought in regard to identifying and meeting different aspects of need prior to attending the group. For example, some young people did not have trainers they could run in, or water bottles to hydrate, etc. There continues to be a need for a system-wide relational response. It is important that the young person be known beyond their identity as an unaccompanied asylum-seeking child. For example, what are their *location* stories? Who are their travelling companions (often other children)? What do they love doing? What do they want us to know about them? What is their relationship to sports?

There are many stories to be explored, discovered, and known that are beyond the dominant discourse held about them (as discussed in previous chapters). As humans, we hold multiple identities that are constantly changing and developing throughout our lives. They are also context- and relational-dependent.

It is only in the doing that we have discovered what works and what doesn't. We have learned about professional cultures and ongoing nudges that need to take place with respect to this type of system-wide response. When using the *relocation* tools, it has been important to review the challenges and dilemmas and to consider how these are linked to all the Macro, Meso and Micro levels.

No full stop to this ending

Coldplay, a UK band, sings about *every new beginning comes from some other beginning's end.*

We feel an affinity for this song, as it links to the idea of time as a circular structure. Time is a circle; it is infinite and unbounded. It is about the return of moments and the flow of lives being lived. The past is changing, and therefore we cannot predict the future (Bakhtin, 1993; Mbembe, 2021; Grimm, 1979).

We started as a small Action Research project in rural Kent. Since then, our understanding of the presenting needs of unaccompanied asylum-seeking children and those who care for them has changed. Their stories and experiences have shaped this change. They have also created hope and new possibilities for other vulnerable children. This learning is now being used with other looked-after children. We believe these children have given, through their stories, the possibility for improved futures for those who have experienced multiple *dislocations*.

Our learning has been that sleep is not singular to a *dislocated* response but rather the journey that shaped patterns of sleep in response to what was required. For instance, drinking lots of energy drinks to stay alert and awake requires translation and transition, from which a new behavioural understanding emerges.

We learned that family goes beyond our genetics.

'We were excited to come together. Myself, along with my co-authors Samantha and Ana, who are my friends, helping me try on wedding dresses for the first time.'
(Elisa, co-author)

Unaccompanied asylum-seeking children experience this fluidity of being family. Their kin are the other young people they are travelling with and others they meet on the journey. We are moved by the stories of kinship we have been told. Those stories are about handing over a lost baby, bundled in your scarf. They are about sleeping in packs and taking turns to be on the outside so that, if attacked, someone stands a chance of survival. They are about sharing your table despite the lack of food. They are about being multi-story individuals and not stuck in an asylum of 'being.' We are the refuge, the place from which *relocation* is an act of intent, an act in which, just like a sleep pack, the welcome takes place.

And just like the young person in Chapter 7, whose name was connected to her family of birth, we would like to continue building bridges from the past to the present in order to walk towards the future.

One of the things we have been vocal about is the need for safe passage. We all need to actively participate in the calling to account of those who prevent safe passage from taking place. This is about giving an account of our abilities; it is accountability. In a briefing by Amnesty International (2021) on safe and legal routes to the UK, it asserts that safe passage requires a visa to be granted or made available for the journey. It is only when there is access to such a system that safe and legal routes can take place. This area is highly complex, and as per the briefing, it is still a contentious issue both in the UK and internationally.

We offered you an invitation to join us in this ongoing journey, and in moving through this book and arriving at this ending chapter, we wonder about the witnessing that might have occurred. We hope you have been able to pause. We hope to receive and hear your voice as an outsider witness. We hope you will go on and develop this framework further. How will it fit with what you are already doing, and how might it change?

In the following poem, we leave you with this connection. We thank you for the many steps we have taken as we walked alongside each other and with you. This is our parting gift, and like all gifts, it may not be what you wanted or expected. Therefore, you might want to re-gift it, throw it away, put it on a shelf, and not look at it again. Yet like some gifts, it might grow on you, connect with you, and be something you use at different times and in different phases.

Life is a journey of knowns and unknowns.
A skip, a hop, a jump, a gunshot of sound in the thump.
The gunshot my heart, your heart, our heart.
Yet it still ticks and becomes the sound of time.
It is fast – a tachycardia of time.
It is slow – a bradycardia of time.
It stops, an arrest of time.
It is in a cycle, a repeat, of a repeat.
It is a rhythmic location.
It is dislocating in its fast, slow and in your arrest.
It is relocating, the new story that restarts the hope.
Yet the asylum awaits.
In the asylum there is madness, solitude,
You are arrested by a loss of story and voice.
A prison of sorts.
In the asylum there is welcome, companions,
A re-membering, recovering, a future dreaming,
A homecoming of sorts.
Well-come to my, your and our heart.
Welcome.

Outsider Witness reflection notes you may want to make about Chapter 9 are as follows:

Take time to consider these questions as a way of connecting to your role, not only as a passive reader but as an 'outsider witness.'

- Can I develop a story about the new perspectives I have connected with in this book?
- What do I want to say to the people who have told their stories in this book?
- In what ways can I honour their stories?
- How and who do I invite to be my 'outsider witnesses'?
- What stories do I want to tell in the future?
- How can I support a way of working relationally?

References

Chapter 1

Akhtar, S. (2001). *Three faces of mourning: Melancholia, manic defence, and moving on.* Jason Aronson Inc.

Alhawsaw, H. Y. (2016). *An incomplete jigsaw puzzle: A narrative study on Arab refugees in Canada.* The University of Western Ontario.

Amnesty International. (2021). *Refugees around the world.* Amnesty International.

Bateson, G. (1972). *Steps to an ecology of mind: Collected essays in anthropology, psychiatry, evolution, and epistemology.* University of Chicago Press.

Bean, T., Derluyn, I., Eurelings-Bontekoe, E., Broekaert, E., & Spinhoven, P. (2007). Validation of the multiple language versions of the reactions to traumatic stress questionnaire. *Journal of Traumatic Stress, 19,* 241–255.

Betancourt, T. S., Newnham, E. A., Layne, C. M., Kim, S., Steinberg, A. M., Ellis, H., & Birman, D. (2012). Trauma history and psychopathology in war-affected refugee children referred for trauma-related mental health services in the United States. *Journal Traumatic Stress, 25*(6), 682–690.

Bhugra, D. (2004). *Migration and mental health.* Wiley Online Library.

Björn, G. (1996). *Development and the social sciences: An uneasy relationship.* John Benjamins Publishing Company.

Bland, A. M., & Derobertis, E. M. (2019). Humanistic perspectives. In V. Zeigler-Hill & T. K. Shackelford (Eds.), *Encyclopaedia of personality and individual difference.* Springer Nature Switzerland AG.

Carr, H., Hatzidimitriadou, E., & Sango, P. (2017). *Evaluation of the sleep project for unaccompanied asylum-seeking children in Kent.* Canterbury Christ Church University.

Dansokho, M. (2016). *Unaccompanied asylum-seeking children–health and wellbeing needs assessment.* Public Health, Halton Borough Council. See unaccompanied-asylum-seeking-children--health-and-wellbeing-needs-assessments--halton-merseysid.pdf (ljmu.ac.uk)

Deluca, L. A., Mcewen, M. M., & Keim, S. M. (2010). United States-Mexico border crossing: Experiences and risk perceptions of undocumented male immigrants. *Journal of Immigrant and Minority Health, 12,* 113–123.

Department for Education. (2019). *Children looked after in England (including adoption),* Year Ending March 31, 2019. GOV.UK (www.gov.uk)

Derluyn, I., & Broekaert, E. (2007). Different perspectives on emotional and behavioural problems in unaccompanied refugee children and adolescents. *Ethnicity Health, 12,* 141–162.

Draper, A., & Hannah, C. (2008). How to create a therapeutic space that enables new under-standing to emerge: Therapeutic conversations with the terminally ill and their families. *Journal of Systemic Therapy, 27*(2), 20–32.

Draper, A., & Marcellino, E. (2020). An early intervention framework for emotional health and wellbeing of unaccompanied minors. In D. Bhugra (Ed.), *Oxford textbook of migrant psychiatry* (Chapter 68, pp. 589–596). Oxford University Press.

English, P., & Mann, B. (2021). *What concerns the British public about immigration policy?* Policy and Current Affairs.

Fazel, M., Reed, R. V., Panter-Brick, C., & Stein, A. (2012, January 21). Mental health of displaced and refugee children resettled in high-income countries: Risk and protective factors. *Lancet, 379*(9812), 266–282.

Given-Wilson, Z., Herlihy, J., & Hodes, M. (2016). Telling the story: A psychological review on assessing adolescents' asylum claims. *Canadian Psychology/Psychologie Canadienne, 57*, 265–273.

Given-Wilson, Z., Hodes, M., & Herlihy, J. (2017). A review of adolescent autobiographical memory and the implications for assessment of unaccompanied minors' refugee determinations. *Clinical Child Psychology and Psychiatry, 23*.

Hagström, A., Hollander, A. C., & Mittendorfer-Rutz, E. (2018). *Mapping of self-harm, suicide attempt, suicide and other mortality in unaccompanied minors seeking asylum in Sweden.* Karolinska Institutet. ISBN: 978-91-7676-052-9.

Henry, H. M., Stiles, W. B., & Biran, M. W. (2005). Loss and mourning in immigration: Using the assimilation model to assess continuing bonds with native culture. *Counselling Psychology Quarterly, 18*(2), 109–119.

Heymann, J., Flores-Macias, F., Hayes, J. A., Kennedy, M., Lahaie, C., & Earle, A. (2009). The impact of migration on the well-being of transnational families: New data from sending communities in Mexico. *Community, Work & Family, 12*(1), 91–103. https://doi.org/10.1080/13668800802155704.

Hughes, G., & Rees, N. (2016). Working with vulnerability and resilience for separated children seeking asylum: Towards stories of hope. In S. Barratt & W. Lobatto (Eds.), *Surviving and thriving in care and beyond: Personal and professional perspectives* (pp. 113–134). Karnac Books.

Human Rights Council Advisory Committee, (2016). *Global issue of unaccompanied migrant children and adolescents and human rights: Progress report of the Human Rights Council Advisory Committee.*

Jakobsen, M., Demott, M. A., & Heir, T. (2014). Prevalence of psychiatric disorders among unaccompanied asylum-seeking adolescents in Norway. *Clinical Practice Epidemiology Mental Health, 10*, 53–58.

Jones, J., & Podkul, J. (2012). *Forced from home: The lost boys and girls of central America.* Women Refugee Commission.

Levine, P. A. (2010). *In an unspoken voice: How the body releases trauma and restores goodness.* North Atlantic Books.

Lowen, A. (1994). *Bioenergetics: The revolutionary therapy that uses the language of the body to heal the problems of the mind.* Penguin.

Masocha, S., & Simpson, M. K. (2012). Developing mental health social work for asylum seekers: A proposed model for practice. *Journal of Social Work, 12*(4), 423–443.

Migration Data Portal. (2021). *Child and young migrants.* See Child and Young Migrants Data. migrationdataportal.org

Montgomery, E. (1998). Refugee children from the Middle East. *Scandinavian Journal of Social Medicine. Supplementum, 54*, 1–152.

Montgomery, E., & Foldspang, A. (2001). Traumatic experience and sleep disturbance in refugee children from the Middle East. *The European Journal of Public, 11*(1), 18–22.

134 References

Myerhoff, B. (1982). Life history among the elderly: Performance, visibility and remembering. In J. Ruby (Ed.), *A crack in the mirror. Reflexive perspectives in anthropology.* University of Pennsylvania Press.

Nardone, M., & Correa-Velez, I. (2016). Unpredictability, invisibility and vulnerability: Unaccompanied asylum-seeking minors' journeys to Australia. *Journal of Refugee Studies, 29*(3), 295–314.

Nemoyer, A., Rodrigues, T., & Alvarez, K. (2019). Psychological practice with unaccompanied immigrant minors: Clinical and legal considerations. *Translational Issues in Psychological Science, 5*(1), 4–16.

Pinto, D. (2007). *Interculturele communicatie, een stap verder* [Intercultural communication, a step further]. Bohn Stafleu van Lochem.

Quesada, J., Hart, L. K., & Bourgeois, P. (2011). Structural vulnerability and health: Latino migrant laborers in the United States. *Medical Anthropology, 30*(4), 339–362.

Rehn-Mendoza, N. (2020). *Mental health and well-being of unaccompanied minors a nordic overview.* Nordic Welfare Centre Sweden.

Sandahl, H., Norredam, M., Hjern, A., Asher, H., & Smith Nielsen, S. (2013). Policies of access to healthcare services for accompanied asylum seeking children in the Nordic countries. *Scandinavian Journal of Public Health, 41*, 630–636.

Shotter, J. (1998, January 28). Participatory action research in a new age of distributed learning and multidimensional dialogically discursively structured flexible, decentralised, heterarchical, fluid forms of self-developing organizations. *Work Organization and Europe as a Development Coalition*, Brussels.

Sourander, A. (1998). Behaviour problems and traumatic events of unaccompanied refugee minors. *Child Abuse Neglect, 22*(7), 719–727.

Suárez-Orozco, C., Todorova, I. L., & Louie, J. (2002). Making up for lost time: The experience of separation and reunification among immigrant families. *Family Process, 41*(4), 625–643. https://doi.org/10.1111/j.1545-5300.2002.00625.

Tauvon, K. B. (1998). Principles of psychodrama. In M. Karp, P. Holmes & K. B. Touvon (Eds.), *The handbook of psychodrama* (pp. 29–46). Routledge.

Torbert, W. R. (2001). The practice of action inquiry. In P. Reason & H. Bandbury (Eds.), *Handbook of action research* (pp. 250–260). Sage.

UNCRC. (2019). *Article 12: If I am a refugee, I have the same rights as children born in that country.* UNCRC.

UNICEF. (2015). *Refugee and migrant crisis in Europe – A summary.* UNICEF.

UNICEF. (2021). *Worldwide, about 43.3 million children had been displaced as a consequence of conflict and violence as of the end of 2022.* UNICEF.

The United Nations Convention on the Rights of the Child. (2019). *Adopted and opened for signature, ratification and accession by General Assembly Resolution 44/25 of 20 November, 1989; entry into force 2 September, 1990*, in accordance with Article 49. Convention on the Rights of the Child | OHCHR.

Valdez, E. S., Valdez, L. A., & Sabo, S. (2015). Structural vulnerability among migrating women and children fleeing central America and Mexico: The public health impact of "humanitarian parole". *Frontiers in Public Health, 3*, 163.

Vogt, W. A. (2013). Crossing Mexico: Structural violence and the commodification of undocumented central American migrants. *American Ethnologist, 40*(4), 764–780. https://doi.org/10.1111/amet.12053.

Walther, S., & Fox, H. (2012). Narrative therapy and outsider witness practice: Teachers as a community of acknowledgement. *Educational and Child Psychology, 29*(2).

White, M. (2002, August 23). Definitional ceremony and outsider-witness responses. *Workshop Notes: Dulwich Centre.* www.dulwichcentre.com.au.

Yaglom, M. (1993). Role of psychocultural factors in the adjustment of soviet jewish refugees: Applying kleinian theory of mourning. *Journal of Contemporary Psychotherapy, 23*, 135–145.

Chapter 2

Adams-Westcott, J., Dafforn, T. A., & Sterne, P. (1993). Escaping victim life stories and co-constructing personal agency. In S. Gilligan & R. Price (Eds.), *Therapeutic conversations*. Norton.

American Psychiatric Association. (2013). *Diagnostic and statistical manual of mental disorders (DSM-5)*. Author.

Bateson, G. (1964). *Preface. An anthology of human communication, text and tape by Watzlawick, Paul*. Science and Behavior Books.

Bruszt, L., & Stark, D. (2003). Who counts? Supranational norms and societal needs. *East European Politics and Societies*, *17*(1), 74–82.

Burnham, J. (1992). Approach-method-technique: Making distinctions and connections. *Human Systems: The Journal of Systemic Consultation and Management*, *3*, 3–26.

Burnham, J. (2012). Developments in the Social GGRRAAACCEEESSS: Visible-invisible and voiced-unvoiced. In I. Krause (Ed.), *Culture and reflexivity in systemic psychotherapy: mutual perspectives*. Karnac.

Caizzi, C. (2012). Embodied trauma: Using the subsymbolic mode to access and change script protocol in traumatized adults. *Transactional Analysis Journal*, *42*(3), 165–175.

Casey, E. S. (2001). Between geography and philosophy. *Annals of the Association of American Geographers*, *91*(4), 684.

Connerton, P. (1989). *How society remembers* (p. 20). Cambridge University Press.

Cronen, V. E. (1994). Coordinated management of meaning: Practical theory for the complexities and contradictions of everyday life. In J. Siegfried (Ed.), *The status of common sense in psychology* (pp. 183–207). Ablex Press.

Cronen, V. E., Chen, V., & Pearce, W. B. (1988). Coordinated management of meaning: A critical theory. *International and Intercultural Communication Annual*, *12*, 66–98.

Cronen, V. E., & Lang, P. (1994). Language and action: Wittgenstein and Dewey in the practice of therapy and consultation. *Human Systems*, *5*(1–2), 5–43.

Davis, C. (2005, July). Hauntology, spectres and phantoms. *French Studies*, *59*(3), 373–379.

Derrida, J. (1994). *Spectres of marx* (K. Peggy, Trans.). Routledge.

Draper, A. (2018) Working with unaccompanied asylum-seeking children: From dislocation to location of what can be. *Metalogos Systemic Online Journal*. https://metalogos-systemic-therapy-journal.eu/

Draper, A., & Hannah, C. (2008). How to create a therapeutic space that enables new understanding to emerge: Therapeutic conversations with the terminally Ill and their families. *Journal of Systemic Therapy*, *27*(2), 20–32.

Draper, A., & Marcellino, E. (2023a). Location, dislocation, relocation (LDR): A new framework to work with young people who have experienced multiple traumas. *EC Neurology*, *15*(4), 48–52.

Draper, A., & Marcellino, E. (2023b). Location, dislocation and relocation: It's all in the be-coming. *Context*, (188), 26–29.

Draper, A., Marcellino, E., & Ogbonnaya, C. (2022). Continuing bond enquiry with refugees: Bridging the past and future. *Journal of Systemic Therapy. Looked after Children's Special Edition*, *44*, 520–534.

EMDR Institute. (2022). www.emdr.com/what-is-emdr/.

Etchison, M., & Kleist, D. (2000). Review of narrative therapy: Research and utility. *The Family Journal*, *8*(1), 61–66.

Fisher, M. (2012). What is hauntology? *Film Quarterly*, *66*(1), 16–24.

Foucault, M. (2003). *The birth of the clinic: The archeology of medical perception* (A. M. Sheridan, Trans.). Routledge.

Freedman, J., & Combs, G. (1996). *Narrative therapy: The social construction of preferred realities*. W. W. Norton & Co.

Gergen, K. J. (1985). The social constructionist movement in modern psychology. *American Psychologist, 40*(3), 266–275.

Harris, M., Myhill, M., & Walker, J. (2012). Thriving in the challenges of geographical dislocation: A case study of elite Australian footballers. *International Journal of Sports Science, 2*(5), 51–60.

Jensen, A., & Penman, R. (2018). *CMM a brief overview*. CMM Institute.

Johnston, T., & Robinson, P. (2017). *Grief work, continuing bonds and co-creating new stories*. CMMI Fellows.

Kohli, R. K. S. (2011). Working to ensure safety, belonging and success for unaccompanied asylum-seeking children. *Child Abuse Review, 20*(5), 311–323.

Lyotard, J. (1979/1984). *The postmodern condition*. Manchester University Press.

Merscham, C. (2000). Restorying trauma with narrative therapy: Using the Phantom Family. *The Family Journal: Counselling and Therapy for Couples and Families, 8*(3).

Pearce, W. B. (1994). *Interpersonal communication: Making social worlds*. HarperCollins.

Pearce, W. B. (2001). *CMM: Reports from users*. Pearce Associates.

Pearce, W. B., & Cronen, V. E. (1980). *Communication, action, and meaning*. Praeger.

Pearce, W. B., & Pearce, K. A. (1990). Transcendent storytelling: Abilities for systemic practitioners and their clients. *Human Systems, 9*(3–4), 167–185.

Pearce, W. B., & Pearce, K. A. (2004). Taking a communication perspective on dialogue. In R. Anderson, L. A. Baxter & K. N. Cissna (Eds.), *Dialogue theorising difference in communication studies*. Sage Publishing.

Rehn-Mendoza, N. (2020). *Mental health and well-being of unaccompanied minors: A Nordic overview*. Nordic Welfare Centre Sweden. nordicwelfare.org/en/publikationer.

Schwartz, R. C. (1999). Narrative therapy expands and contracts family therapy's horizons. *Journal of Marital and Family Therapy, 25*(2), 263–267.

Straiton, M. L., Aambø, A. K., & Johansen, R. (2019). Perceived discrimination, health and mental health among immigrants in Norway: The role of moderating factors. *BMC Public Health, 19*, 325.

Strong, T. (1995). Clinical languages/clinical realities. *Human Systems: Journal of Systemic Consultation and Management, 6*(1), 53–65.

Tomm, K. (1987a). Interventive interviewing: Part I. Strategizing as a fourth guideline for the therapist. *Family Process, 26*, 2–13.

Tomm, K. (1987b). Interventive interviewing: Part II. Reflexive questioning as a means to enable self-healing. *Family Process, 26*, 153–183.

Tomm, K. (1988). Interventive interviewing: Part III. Intending to ask lineal, circular, reflexive and strategic questions? *Family Process, 27*, 1–15.

Tomm, K. (1990). A critique of the DSM. *Dulwich Centre Newsletter, 3*, 5–8.

Tomm, K. (1991). Beginnings of a 'HIPs and PIPs' approach to psychiatric assessment. *The Calgary Participator, 1*, 21–24.

Tomm, K. (1992). Therapeutic distinctions in an ongoing therapy. In S. McNamee & K. Gergen (Eds.), *Constructing therapy: Social constructionism and the therapeutic process* (pp. 116–135). Sage.

Tomm, K. (1998). A question of perspective. *Journal of Marital and Family Therapy, 24*(4), 409–414.

Tomm, K., George, S., Wulff, D., & Strong, T. (2014). *Patterns in interpersonal interactions: Inviting relational understanding for therapeutic change*. Routledge: Taylor Francis Group.

Watzlawick, P. (1964). An anthology of human communication (Text and Two-hour Tape). By Paul Watzlawick, Ph.D. Preface by Gregory Bateson. In *Science and behaviour books*. Palo Alto, California: Science & Behavior Books, 1964. Pp. vi + 63.

White, C., & Denborough, D. (1998). *Introducing narrative therapy: A collection of practice-based writing*. A Collection of Practice Based Writings Paperback.

White, M. (1995). *Re-authoring lives: Interviews and essays*. Dulwich Centre Publications.
White, M., & Epston, D. (1990). *Narrative means to therapeutic ends* (pp. 184–492). Norton. Transformative Learning Conference, October 23–25, 2003.
Ziminski, J. (2017). A pathway through the Landscape of theory. *Context, 150*, 21–25.

Chapter 3

Anthony, B., Kamaludin, A., Romli, A., Reffei, A. F., Phon, D. N., Abdullah, A., & Ming, G. L. (2022). Blended learning adoption and implementation in higher education: A theoretical and systematic review. *Technology, Knowledge and Learning, 27*, 531–578.
Bean, T., Derluyn, I., Eurelings-Bontekoe, E., Broekaert, E., & Spinhoven, P. (2007, April). Comparing psychological distress, traumatic stress reactions, and experiences of unaccompanied refugee minors with experiences of adolescents accompanied by parents. *Journal of Nervous and Mental Disease, 195*(4), 288–297.
Bellis, M. A., Hughes, K., Leckenby, N., Hardcastle, K. A., Perkins, C., & Lowey, H. (2014). Measuring mortality and the burden of adult disease associated with adverse childhood experiences in England: A national survey. *Journal of Public Health, 37*(3), 445–454.
Bick, J., & Nelson, C. (2016). Early adverse experiences and the developing brain. *Neuropsychopharmacol, 41*, 177–196.
Black, J. E., & Greenough, W. T. (1986). Induction of pattern in neural structure by experience, Implications for cognitive development. In M. E. Lamb, A. L. Brown & B. Rogoff (Eds.), *Advances in developmental psychology* (Vol. 4, pp. 1–50). Lawrence Earlbaum Assoc.
Bohacek, J., & Mansuy, I. M. (2015, November). Molecular insights into transgenerational non-genetic inheritance of acquired behaviours. *Nature Reviews Genetics, 16*(11), 641–652.
Bremner, J. D. (2006). Traumatic stress: Effects on the brain. *Dialogues in Clinical Neuroscience, 8*(4), 445–461.
Clarke, H. J., & Vieux, K. F. (2015). Epigenetic inheritance through the female germ-line: The known, the unknown, and the possible. *Seminars in Cell & Developmental Biology, 43*, 106–116.
De Bellis, M. D., & Zlsk, A. (2014). The biological effects of childhood trauma. *Child and Adolescent Psychiatric Clinics of North America, 23*(2), 185–222.
De Gruy, L. J. (2005). *Post traumatic slave syndrome: America's legacy of enduring injury and healing*. Uptone Press.
Doidge, N. (2007). *The brain that changes itself: Stories of personal triumph from the frontiers of brain science* (Reprint ed.). Penguin Books.
Eyerman, R. (2001). *Cultural trauma: Slavery and the formation of African American identity*. Cambridge University Press.
Felitti, V. J., Anda, R. F., Nordenberg, D., Williamson, D. F., Spitz, A. M., Edwards, V., Koss, M. P., & Marks, J. S. (1998). Relationship of childhood abuse and household dysfunction to many of the leading causes of death in adults: The adverse childhood experiences (ACE) study. *American Journal of Preventive Medicine, 14*(4), 245–258.
Gatt, J., Nemeroff, C., Dobson-Stone, C., Paul, R., Bryant, R., Schofield, P., & Williams, L. (2009). Interactions between bdnf val66met polymorphism and early life stress predict brain and arousal pathways to syndromal depression and anxiety. *Molecular Psychiatry, 14*(7), 681.
Goodkind, M., Eickhoff, S. B., Oathes, D. J., Jiang, Y., Chang, A., Jones-Hagata, L. B., & Korgaonkar, M. S. (2015). Identification of a common neurobiological substrate for mental illness. *JAMA Psychiatry, 72*(4), 305–315.
Greenough, W. T., & Black, J. E. (1992). Induction of brain structure by experience: Substrates for cognitive development. In M. R. Gunnar & C. A. Nelson (Eds.), *Developmental behavioural neuroscience* (pp. 155–200). Lawrence Erlbaum Associates, Inc.

Greenough, W. T., Black, J. E., & Wallace, C. S. (1987). Experience and brain development. *Child Development, 58*(3), 539–559.

Haas, B. W., & Canli, T. (2008). Emotional memory function, personality structure and psychopathology: A neural system approach to the identification of vulnerability markers. *Brain Research Reviews, 58*(1), 71–84.

Hackman, D. A., Farah, M. J., & Meaney, M. J. (2010). Socioeconomic status and the brain: Mechanistic insights from human and animal research. *Nature Reviews Neuroscience, 11*(9), 651.

Hambrick, D. Z., Burgoyne, A. P., Macnamara, B. N., & Ullén, F. (2018, February 15). Toward a multifactorial model of expertise: Beyond born versus made. *Annals of the New York Academy of Sciences.* http://doi.org/10.1111/nyas.13586. Epub ahead of print. PMID: 29446457.

Hanson, J. L., Nacewicz, B. M., Sutterer, M. J., Cayo, A. A., Schaefer, S. M., Rudolph, K. D., Shirtcliff, E. A., Pollak, S. D., & Davidson, R. J. (2015, February 15). Behavioral problems after early life stress: Contributions of the hippocampus and amygdala. *Biological Psychiatry, 77*(4), 314–323.

Harrison, N. A., & Critchley, H. D. (2007). Affective neuroscience and psychiatry. *British Journal of Psychiatry, 191*, 192–194.

Hirsch, H. V. B., & Spinelli, D. N. (1970). Visual experience modifies distribution of horizontally and vertically oriented receptive fields in cats. *Science, 168*, 869–871.

Hubel, D. H., & Wiesel, T. N. (1970). The period of susceptibility to the physiological effects of unilateral eye closure in kittens. *The Journal Physiology (London), 206*, 419–436.

Hughes, K., Bellis, M., Hardcastle, K., Sethi, D., Butchart, A., Mikton, C., Jones, L., & Dunne, M. (2017, August). The effect of multiple adverse childhood experiences on health: A systematic review and meta-analysis. *Lancet, Public Health, 2*(8), 356–366.

James, W. (1890). *The principles of psychology* (Vols. 1–2).

McLaughlin, K. A., Sheridan, M. A., & Lambert, H. K. (2014, November). Childhood adversity and neural development: Deprivation and threat as distinct dimensions of early experience. *Neuroscience Biobehavioral Reviews, 47*, 578–591.

Murdock, A. (2020). *The evolutionary advantage of the teenage brain.* University of California.

Nicolson, K. P., Mills, S. E. E., Senaratne, D. N. S., Colvin, L. A., & Smith, B. H. (2023). What is the association between childhood adversity and subsequent chronic pain in adulthood? A systematic review. *BJA Open, 6*.

Oshri, A., Gray, J. C., Owens, M. M., Liu, S., Duprey, E. B., Sweet, L. H., & MacKillop, J. (2019, November). Adverse childhood experiences and amygdalar reduction: High-resolution segmentation reveals associations with subnuclei and psychiatric outcomes. *Child Maltreatment, 24*(4), 400–410.

O'Toole, P. W., Marchesi, J. R., & Hill, C. (2017). Next-generation probiotics: The spectrum from probiotics to live biotherapeutics. *Nature Microbiology, 2*, 17057.

Puderbaugh, M., & Emmady, P. D. (2022). *Neuroplasticity.* StatPearls Publishing.

Rakoff, V., Signal, J. J., & Epstein, N. (1966). Children and families of concentration camp survivors. *Canada's Mental Health, 14*, 24–26.

Ridout, K. K., Levandowski, M., Ridout, S. J., Gantz, L., Goonan, K., Palermo, D., Price, L. H., & Tyrka, A. R. (2018). Early life adversity and telomere length: A meta-analysis. *Molecular Psychiatry, 23*(4), 858–871.

Spinelli, D. N. (1970). Distribution of receptive field orientation: Modification contingent on conditions of visual experience. *Science, 168*, 869–871.

Teicher, M. H., & Samson, J. A. (2016). Annual research review: Enduring neurobiological effects of childhood abuse and neglect. *Journal of Child Psychology and Psychiatry, 57*(3), 241–266. https://doi.org/10.1111/jcpp.12507

Van Der Kolk, B. (2014). *The body keeps the score: Mind, brain and body in the transformation of trauma*. Penguin.

Walker, P. (2013). *Complex PTSD: From surviving to thriving: A guide and map for recovering from childhood trauma*. Azure Coyote Publishing.

Wiese, E. B., & Burhorst, I. (2007). The mental health of asylum-seeking and refugee children and adolescents attending a clinic in the Netherlands. *Transcultural Psychiatry*, *44*(4), 596–613.

Yehuda, R., & Bierer, L. M. (2009). The relevance of epigenetics to PTSD: Implications for the DSM-V. *Journal of Traumatic Stress*, *22*(5), 427–434.

Chapter 4

American Psychiatric Association. (2013). *Diagnostic and statistical manual of mental disorders* (5th ed.). American Psychiatric Association.

Bean, T., Derluyn, I., Eurelings-Bontekoe, E., Broekaert, E., & Spinhoven, P. (2007). Comparing psychological distress, traumatic stress reactions, and experiences of unaccompanied refugee minors with experiences of adolescents accompanied by parents. *The Journal of Nervous and Mental Disease*, *195*(4), 288–297.

Bentovim, A., Jolliffe, C., Draper, A., & Marcellino, E. (2023). *Trauma and looked after children*, Short lectures for the Association of Children's and Adolescent Mental Health Services in collaboration with Child and Family Training and Improved Futures.

Burnham, J. (2012). Developments in social GGRRRAAACCEEESSS: Visible-invisible and voiced-unvoiced. In I.-B. Krause (Ed.), *Cultural reflexivity*. Karnac.

Children's Society. (2018). *Distress signals: Unaccompanied young people's struggle for mental health*. Children's Society.

Copeland, W. E., Keeler, G., Angold, A., & Costello, E. J. (2007). Traumatic events and posttraumatic stress in childhood. *Archives of General Psychiatry*, *64*(5), 577–584.

Crandon, L. (1983). Why Susto? *Ethnology*, *22*(2), 153–167.

Dalgleish, T., Black, M., Johnston, D., & Bevan, A. (2020). Transdiagnostic approaches to mental health problems: Current status and future directions. *Journal of Consulting and Clinical Psychology*, *88*(3), 179–195

Danese, A. (2019). Annual research review: Rethinking childhood trauma-new research directions for measurement, study design and analytical strategies. *The Journal of Child Psychology and Psychiatry*, *61*(3).

de Shazer, S. (1991). *Putting differences to work*. Norton.

de Shazer, S., & Berg, I. K. (1995). The brief therapy tradition. In J. Weakland & W. Ray (Eds.), *Propagations: Thirty years of influence from the mental research institute*. The Haworth Press.

de Shazer, S., & Dolan, Y., with Korman, H., Trepper, T., McCollum, E., & Kim Berg, I. (2007). *More than miracles. The state of the art of solution focused brief therapy*. Routledge.

Donovan, K. A., Handzo, G., Corbett, C., Vanderlan, J., Brewer, B. W., & Ahmed, K. (2022). NCCN distress thermometer problem list update. *Journal of the National Comprehensive Cancer Network*, *20*(1), 96–98.

Draper, A., & Marcellino, E. (2020). An early intervention framework for emotional health and wellbeing of unaccompanied minors. In D. Bhugra (Ed.), *Oxford textbook of migrant psychiatry* (Chapter 68, pp. 589–596). Oxford University Press.

Draper, A., Marcellino, E., Benham, K., & Dunn, Z. (2023). The distress screening tool: An outcome measure in the work with looked after children and unaccompanied asylum-seeking minors. *EC Neurology Journal*, *15*(3).

Evans, S., & Santucci, L. (2021, July). A modular, transdiagnostic approach to treating severe irritability in children and adolescents. *Child and Adolescent Psychiatry Clinics*, *30*(3), 623–636.

Fisch, R., & Schlanger, K. (1999). *Brief therapy with intimidating cases: Changing the unchangeable*. Jossey-Bass.

Fisch, R., Weakland, J. H., & Segal, L. (1982). *The tactics of change: Doing therapy briefly*. Jossey-Bass.

Graham-Wisener, L. (2021). Validation of the distress thermometer in patients with advanced cancer receiving specialist palliative care in a hospice setting. *Palliative Medicine, 35*(1), 120–129.

Greene, R. N. (2019). Kinship, friendship, and service provider social ties and how they influence well-being among newly resettled refugees. *American Sociological Association. Socius: Sociological Research for a Dynamic World, 5*, 1–11.

Hanson, J. L., Nacewicz, B. M., Sutterer, M. J., Cayo, A. A., Schaefer, S. M., Rudolph, K. D., & Davidson, R. J. (2015). Behavioral problems after early life stress: Contributions of the hippocampus and amygdala. *Biological Psychiatry, 77*(4), 314–323.

Harvard University Centre of the Developing Child. (2023). Key concepts in Brain Architecture.

Jackson, D. D. (1967). Theory. In P. Watzlawick & J. H. Weakland (Eds.), *The interactional view* (pp. 1–21). Norton.

Knight, M., et al. (2021). *Saving lives, improving mothers' care rapid report 2021: Learning from SARSCoV-2-related and associated maternal deaths in the UK, June 2021–March 2021*. National Perinatal Epidemiology Unit, University of Oxford.

Krause, I.-G. (1989). Sining heart: A punjabi communication of distress. *Social Science and Medicine, 29*(4), 563–575.

Lazenby, M., Tan, H., Pasacreta, N., Ercolano, E., & McCorkle, R. (2015). The five steps of comprehensive psychosocial distress screening. *Current Oncology Reports, 17*(5), 447.

Lim, N. (2016). Cultural differences in emotion: Differences in emotional arousal level between the East and the West. *Integrative Medicine Research, 5*(2), 105–109.

Lovering, N. (2022). *Healing from childhood trauma: Effects, healing and EMDR*. PsychCentral.

Mittendorfer-Rutz, E., Hagström, A., & Hollander, A. C. (2019). High suicide rates among unaccompanied minors/youth seeking asylum in Sweden. *Crisis, 41*(4), 314–317.

Montori, V. M., Ruissen, M. M., Hargraves, I. G., & Kunneman, M. (2023). Shared decision-making as a method of care. *BMJ Evidence-Based Medicine, 28*, 213–217.

National Comprehensive Cancer Network. (2020). *Guide for distressed patients during cancer care*. See NCCN Guidelines for Patients Distress During Cancer Care.

Nichter, M. P. (1981). Idioms of distress: Alternatives in the expression of psychosocial distress: A case study from South India. *Culture Medicine Psychiatry, 5*, 379–408.

Nichter, M. P. (2010). Idioms of distress revisited. *Culture Medicine Psychiatry, 34*(2), 401–416.

Nichols, M. P., & Schwartz, R. C. (2008). *Family therapy: Concepts and methods* (7th ed.). Pearson.

Ownby, K. K. (2019, March). Use of the distress thermometer in clinical practice. *Journal of Advanced Practitioner in Oncology, 10*(2), 175–179.

Tian, T., Li, J., Zhang, G., Wang, J., Liu, D., Wan, C., Fang, J., Wu, D., Zhou, Y., & Zhu, W. (2021). Effects of childhood trauma experience and BDNF val66met polymorphism on brain plasticity related to emotion regulation. *Behavioural Brain Research, 398*(21), 112949.

World Health Organisation. (2004). *Prevention of mental disorders; Effective interventions and policy options*. World Health Organisation.

Youth Government. (2022). *Youth with increased risk of suicide*. Youth Government.

Chapter 5

Aronen, E. T., Paavonen, E. J., Fjällberg, M., Soininen, M., & Törrönen, J. (2000). Sleep and psychiatric symptoms in school-age children. *Journal of the American Academy of Child & Adolescent Psychiatry, 39*(4), 502–508.

Awad, K. M., Drescher, A. A., Malhotra, A., & Quan, S. F. (2013). Effects of exercise and nutritional intake on sleep architecture in adolescents. *Sleep Breath, 17*, 117–124.

Bean, T., Derluyn, I., Eurelings-Bontekoe, E., Broekaert, E., & Spinhoven, P. (2007). Comparing psychological distress, traumatic stress reactions, and experiences of unaccompanied refugee minors with experiences of adolescents accompanied by parents. *The Journal of Nervous and Mental Disease, 195*(4), 288–297.

Benoit, D., Zeanah, C. H., Boucher, C., & Minde, K. K. (1992). Sleep disorders in early childhood: Association with insecure maternal attachment. *Journal of the American Academy of Child & Adolescent Psychiatry, 31*(1), 86–93.

Bhugra, D. (2004). Migration, distress and cultural identity. *British Medical Bulletin, 69*, 129–141.

Bronstein, I., & Montgomery, P. (2013). Sleeping patterns of Afghan unaccompanied asylum-seeking adolescents: A large observational study. *PLoS ONE, 8*(2), e56156.

Cardinali, D. P., Brown, G. M., & Pandi-Perumal, S. R. (2021). Chapter 24–chronotherapy. *Handbook of Clinical Neurology, 179*, 357–370.

Carr, H., Hatzidimitriadou, E., & Sango, P. (2017). Evaluation of the sleep project for unaccompanied asylum-seeking children in kent. *European Journal of Public Health [online], 28*(1), 70.

Dore-Stites, D. (2017). Delayed sleep wake phase disorder in adolescents: Chronotherapy and best practices. *Psychiatric Times.*

Draper, A. (2016). *An action research project final report looking at the emotional health and wellbeing needs of unaccompanied asylum-seeking children in Kent.* Unpublished report.

Elliott, A., & McMahon, C. (2011). Anxiety among an Australian sample of young girls adopted from China. *Adoption Quarterly, 14*(3), 161–180.

Elphick, H. E., Lawson, C., Ives, A., Siddall, S., Kingshott, R. N., Reynolds, J., Dawson, V., & Hall, L. (2019). Pilot study of an integrated model of sleep support for children: A before and after evaluation. *BMJ Paediatrics Open, 3*, e000551. https://doi.org/10.1136/bmjpo-2019-000551

Fusco, R. A., & Kulkarni, S. J. (2018). Bedtime is when bad stuff happens: Sleep problems in foster care alumni. *Children and Youth Services Review, 95*, 42–48

Gregory, A. M., & Sadeh, A. (2012). Sleep, emotional and behavioural difficulties in children and adolescents, *Sleep Medicine Reviews, 16*(2), 129–136.

Hambrick, E. P. (2017). Do sleep problems mediate the link between adverse childhood experiences (ACE) and delinquency in preadolescent children in foster care? *The Journal of Child Psychology and Psychiatry, 59*(2), 140–149.

Harvey, A. G., Jones, C., & Schmidt, D. A. (2003). Sleep and posttraumatic stress disorder: A review. *Clinical Psychology Review, 23*(3), 377–407.

Johnson, E. O., Chilcoat, H. D., & Breslau, N. (2000). Trouble sleeping and anxiety/depression in childhood. *Psychiatry Research, 94*(2), 93–102.

Lawrence, H., & Michelmorel, O. (2019). *Understanding sleep problems experienced by unaccompanied asylum-seeking children and children in care. A rapid review.* Coram.

Levitan, R. D. (2005). What is the optimal implementation of bright light therapy for seasonal affective disorder (SAD)? *Journal Psychiatry Neuroscience, 30*(1), 72.

Marsh, S. (2020). Sharp rise in hospital admissions for children with sleep disorders. *The Guardian.*

Montgomery, E. (2011). Trauma, exile and mental health in young refugees. *Acta Psychiatrica Scandinavica, 124*(440), 1–35.

Montgomery, E., & Foldspang, A. (2001). Traumatic experience and sleep disturbance in refugee children from the Middle East. *European Journal of Public Health*, *11*(1), 18–22.

National Health Service. (2022). www.nhs.uk/live-well/sleep-and-tiredness/why-lack-of-sleep-is-bad-for-your-health/

The National Sleep Foundation. (2022). *The national sleep foundation's sleep in America poll Americans can do more during the day to help their sleep at night.* See National Sleep Foundation. thensf.org.

Pail, G., Huf, W., Pjrek, E., Winkler, D., Willeit, M., Praschak-Rieder, N., & Kasper, S. (2011). Bright-light therapy in the treatment of mood disorders. *Neuropsychobiology*, *64*(3), 152–162.

Pilcher, J. J., & Huffcutt, A. I. (1996). Effects of sleep deprivation on performance: A meta-analysis. *Sleep*, *19*(4), 318–326.

Praschak-Rieder, N., & Willeit, M. (2003). Treatment of seasonal affective disorders. *Dialogues Clinical Neuroscience*, *5*(4), 389–398.

Rajaprakash, M., Kerr, E., Friedlander, B., & Weiss, S. (2017). Sleep disorders in a sample of adopted children: A pilot study. *Children*, *4*(9), 77

Sundelin, T., Lekander, M., Sorjonen, K., & Axelsson, J. (2017, May 17). Negative effects of restricted sleep on facial appearance and social appeal. *Royal Society Open Science*, *4*(5), 160918.

Tininenko, J., Fisher, P. A., Bruce, J., & Pears, K. C. (2010). Sleep disruption in young foster children. *Child Psychiatry and Human Development [online]*, *41*(4), 409–424.

Vorona, R. D., Winn, M. P., Babineau, T. W., Eng, B. P., Feldman, H. R., & Ware, J. C. (2005). Overweight and obese patients in a primary care population report less sleep than patients with a normal body mass index. *Archives of Internal Medicine*, *165*(1), 25–30.

Vriend, J., & Corkum, P. (2011). Clinical management of behavioural insomnia of childhood. *Psychology Research and Behaviour Management*, *4*, 69.

Wiese, E. B., & Burhorst, I. (2007). The mental health of asylum-seeking and refugee children and adolescents attending a clinic in the Netherlands. *Transcultural Psychiatry*, *44*(4), 596–613.

Chapter 6

Beagan, B. L., & Chapman, G. E. (2012). Meanings of food, eating and health among African Nova Scotians: Certain things aren't meant for Black folk. *Ethnicity and Health*, *17*, 513.

Breit, S., Kupferberg, A., Rogler, G., & Hasler, G. (2018). Vagus nerve as modulator of the brain – gut axis in psychiatric and inflammatory disorders. *Frontiers in Psychiatry, Secope: Psychological Therapy and Psychosomatics*, *9*, 44.

Browne, S. J. (2021). What the vagus nerve is and how to stimulate it for better mental health. *Forbes online*.

Bruce, L. J., & Ricciardelli, L. A. (2015). A systematic review of the psychosocial correlates of intuitive eating among adult women. *Appetite*, *96*, 454–472.

Burnham, J. (2012). Developments in the social GGRRAAACCEEESSS: Visible-invisible and voiced-unvoiced. In I. Krause (Ed.), *Culture and reflexivity in systemic psychotherapy: Mutual perspectives*. Karnac.

Cohen, A. B. (2021). You can learn a lot about religion from food. *Current Opinion in Psychology*, *40*, 1–5.

Culbert, K. M., Racine, S. E., & Klump, K. L. (2016). Hormonal factors and disturbances in eating disorders. *Current Psychiatry Reports*, *18*, 65.

Del Toro-Barbosa, M., Hurtado-Romero, A., Garcia-Amezquita, L. E., & García-Cayuela, T. (2020, December 19). Psychobiotics: Mechanisms of action, evaluation methods and effectiveness in applications with food products. *Nutrients*, *12*(12), 3896.

Descilo, T., Vedamurtachar, A., Gerbarg, P. L., Nagaraja, D., Gangadhar, B. N., Damodaran, B., et al. (2010). Effects of a yoga breath intervention alone and in combination with an exposure therapy for post-traumatic stress disorder and depression in survivors of the 2004 South-East Asia tsunami. *Acta Psychiatrica Scandinavica, 121*, 289–300.

Draper, A. (2012). The repercussions of baked beans – can routine be a way parentally bereaved children construct a durable biography? *Bereavement Care Journal, 31*(2).

Draper, A. (2020). *New perspectives of UASC health and interventions: Beyond post-traumatic stress disorder*. Coram.

Ekstrand, B., Scheers, N., Rasmussen, M. K., Young, J. F., Ross, A. B., & Landberg, R. (2021). Brain foods – the role of diet in brain performance and health. *Nutrition Reviews, 79*(6), 693–708.

Forestell, C. A., & Mennella, J. A. (2015). The ontogeny of taste perception and preference throughout childhood. In R. L. Doty (Ed.), *Handbook of olfaction and gustation* (3rd ed.). Marcel Dekker.

Fox, R. (2003). *Food and eating: an anthropological perspective*. Social Issues Research Centre.

Fuller, R. (1989). Probiotics in man and animals. *Journal of Applied Bacteriology, 66*(5), 365–378.

Glanz, K., Basil, M., Maibach, E., Goldberg, J., & Snyder, D. (1998). Why Americans eat what they do: Taste, nutrition, cost, convenience, and weight control concerns as influences on food consumption. *Journal American Dietetic Association, 98*, 1118–1126.

Holtzman, J. D. (2006, October). Food and memory. *Annual Review of Anthropology, 35*, 361–378.

Keys, A., Brozek, J., Henshel, A., Mickelson, O., & Taylor, H. L. (1950). *The biology of human starvation* (Vols. 1–2). University of Minnesota Press.

Khalesi, S., Bellissimo, N., Vandelanotte, C., Williams, S., Stanley, D., & Irwin, C. (2019). A review of probiotic supplementation in healthy adults: Helpful or hype? *European Journal Clinical Nutrition, 73*(1), 24–37.

Khalsa, S. S., Craske, M. G., Li, W., Vangala, S., Strober, M., & Feusner, J. D. (2015). Altered interoceptive awareness in anorexia nervosa: Effects of meal anticipation, consumption and bodily arousal. *International Journal Eating Disorders, 48*, 889–897.

Kim, C. S., Cha, L., Sim, M., Jung, S., Chun, W. Y., Baik, H. W., & Shin, D. M. (2021). Probiotic supplementation improves cognitive function and mood with changes in gut microbiota in community-dwelling older adults: A randomized, double-blind, placebo-controlled, multicenter trial. *Journal Gerontology A Biological Sciences Medical Science, 76*(1), 32–40.

Linardon, J., & Mitchell, S. (2017). Rigid dietary control, flexible dietary control, and intuitive eating: Evidence for their differential relationship to disordered eating and body image concerns. *Eating Behaviours, 26*, 16–22.

MacCormack, J. K., & Lindquist, K. A. (2019, March). Feeling hangry? When hunger is conceptualized as emotion. *Emotion, 19*(2), 301–319.

Parasecoli, F. (2011). Savoring semiotics: Food in intercultural communication. *Social Semiotics, 21*, 645.

Schoenefeld, S. J., & Webb, J. B. (2013). Self-compassion and intuitive eating in college women: Examining the contributions of distress tolerance and body image acceptance and action. *Eating Behaviors, 14*(4), 493–496.

Selhub, E. (2022). *Nutritional psychiatry: Your brain on food*. Harvard Health Blog.

Shahrokhi, M., & Nagalli, S. (2023). Probiotics. In *StatPearls*. StatPearls Publishing.

Steiner, J. E., Glaser, D., Hawilo, M. E., & Berridge, K. C. (2001, January). Comparative expression of hedonic impact: Affective reactions to taste by human infants and other primates. *Neuroscience Biobehavioral Reviews, 25*(1), 53–74.

Tschop, M., Smiley, D. L., & Heiman, M. L. (2000). Ghrelin induces adiposity in rodents. *Nature, 407*, 908–913

Tyagi, A., & Cohen, M. (2016). Yoga and heart rate variability: A comprehensive review of the literature. *International Journal Yoga, 9,* 97–113.

Tylka, T. L., Calogero, R. M., & Daníelsdóttir, S. (2015). Is intuitive eating the same as flexible dietary control? Their links to each other and well-being could provide an answer. *Appetite, 95,* 166–175.

Waxenbaum, J. A., Reddy, V., & Varacallo, M. (2022). *Anatomy, autonomic nervous system.* National Library of Medicine.

Wood, N. R. (2012). Recipes for life. *International Journal of Narrative Therapy & Community Work, 2,* 34–43.

Chapter 7

Bakhtin, M. M. (1993). *Towards a philosophy of the act* (V. Liapunov, Ed.). University of Texas Press.

Bhugra, D., & Becker, M. A. (2005). Migration, cultural bereavement and cultural identity. *World Psychiatry, 4*(1), 18–24.

Bowlby, J. (1980). *Attachment and loss: Loss, sadness and depression* (Vol. 3). Basic.

Draper, A. (2009). *Hope in palliative care.* Context.

Draper, A., & Marcellino, E. (2023). *Continuing bonds enquiry: When your name is trafficked.* Child Psychotherapy Matters.

Draper, A., Marcellino, E., & Ogbonnaya, C. (2022). Continuing bonds enquiry with refugees: Bridging the past and the future. *Journal of Family Therapy, 44*(4).

Freud, S. (1957). Mourning and melancholia. In J. Strachey (Ed. & Trans.), *Standard edition of the complete psychological works of Sigmund Freud* (pp. 152–170). Hogarth Press.

Grimm, R. H. (1979). Circularity and self-reference in Nietzsche. *Metaphilosophy, 10,* 289–305.

Hedtke, L. (2000). Dancing with death. *Gecko: A Journal of Deconstruction and Narrative Ideas in Therapeutic Practice, 2,* 3–14.

Hedtke, L. (2001). Stories of living and dying. *Gecko: A Journal of Deconstruction and Narrative Ideas in Therapeutic Practice, 1,* 4–27.

Hedtke, L., & Winslade, J. (2004). *Re-membering lives: Conversations with the dying and the bereaved.* Baywood.

Ibler, R. A. (2019). *Cultural memory.* Springer.

Klass, D. (2018). *Continuing Bonds in bereavement. New Directions for research and practice.* Routledge.

Klass, D., & Chow, A. Y. M. (2011). Culture and ethnicity in experiencing, policing, and handling grief. In R. A. Neimeyer, D. L. Harris, H. R. Winokuer & G. F. Thornton (Eds.), *Grief and bereavement in contemporary society: Bridging research and practice* (1st ed., pp. 341–354). Routledge.

Klass, D., Silverman, P. R., & Nickman, S. (Eds.). (1996). *Continuing bonds: New understandings of grief* (1st ed.). Taylor & Francis.

Laenui, P. (2000). Process of decolonization. In M. Battiste (Ed.), *Reclaiming indigenous voice and vision* (pp. 156–160). UBC Press.

Machiavelli, N. (1953). *The prince.* Penguin Books. Translated with Notes by George Bull in 2006.

Mbembe, A. (2021). *Out of the dark night: Essays on decolonization.* Columbia University Press.

Myerhoff, B. (1982). Life history among the elderly: Performance, visibility and remembering. In J. Ruby (Ed.), *A crack in the mirror: Reflexive perspectives in anthropology* (pp. 99–117). University of Pennsylvania Press.

Pearce, W. B., & Pearce, K. A. (1990). Transcendent storytelling: Abilities for systemic practitioners and their clients. *Human Systems, 9*(3–4), 167–185.

Rice, R. H. (2015). Narrative therapy. *The SAGE Encyclopedia of Theory in Counseling and Psychology*, *2*, 695.

Silverman, P., & Klass, D. (1996). Introduction: What's the problem? In D. Klass, P. Silverman & S. Nickman (Eds.), *Continuing bonds: New understandings of grief* (pp. 3–27). American Psychological Association Press.

White, M. (1988). Saying hullo again: The incorporation of the lost relationship in the resolution of grief. *Dulwich Centre Newsletter*, *3*, 29–36.

White, M. (2007). *Maps of narrative practice*. W. W. Norton & Co.

Chapter 8

Allcock, A. (2019). *Healing environments for children who have experienced trauma*. ESSS Outlines.

Amano, T., & Toichi, M. (2016, October 12). The role of alternating bilateral stimulation in establishing positive cognition in EMDR therapy: A multi-channel near-infrared spectroscopy study. *PLoS ONE*, *11*(10), e0162735.

Basso, J., & Suzuki, W. A. (2017). The effects of acute exercise on mood, cognition, neurophysiology, and neurochemical pathways: A review. *Brain Plasticity*, *2*, 127–152.

Cooper, C., Moon, H. Y., & van Praag, H. (2017). On the run for hippocampal plasticity. Cold Spring Harbor Lab Perspectives in Medicine. In J. R. Zierath, M. J. Joyner & M. A. Hawley (Eds.), *The biology of exercise*. CSHL Press.

Dale, L. P., Vanderloo, L., Moore, S., & Faulkner, G. (2019). Physical activity and depression, anxiety, and self-esteem in children and youth: An umbrella systematic review. *Mental Health and Physical Activity*, *16*, 66–79.

De Jongh, A., Ernst, R., Marques, L., & Hornsveld, H. (2013). The impact of eye movements and tones on disturbing memories involving PTSD and other mental disorders. *Journal of Behavior Therapy and Experimental Psychiatry*, *44*, 477–483.

Dolezal, B. A., Neufeld, E. V., Boland, D. M., Martin, J. L., & Cooper, C. B. (2017). Interrelationship between sleep and exercise: A systematic review. *Advances in Preventive Medicine*, *2017*, 1364387.

Draper, A., Marcellino, E., Benham, K., & Dunn, Z. D. (2023). Fast feet forward: A sports group for looked- after children and unaccompanied asylum-seeking children as an early intervention to process trauma and reduce distress. *Counselling and Psychotherapy Research*, *24*(1), 342–351.

Draper, A., Marcellino, E., & Ogbonnaya, C. (2020). Fast feet forward: Sports training and running practice to reduce stress and increase positive cognitions in unaccompanied asylum-seeking minors. *Counselling and Psychotherapy Research*, *20*(4), 638–646.

Draper, A., Marcellino, E., & Ogbonnaya, C. (2021). Fast feet forward: Early intervention protocol using bilateral movements to reduce stress and increase positive cognitions in adopted children with complex trauma presentation. *Counselling and Psychotherapy Research*, *22*(3).

Duzel, E., van Praag, H., & Sendtner, M. (2016). Can physical exercise in old age improve memory and hippocampal function? *Brain*, *139*, 662–673.

Engelhard, I. M., van Uijen, S. L., & Van Den Hout, M. A. (2010b). The impact of taxing working memory on negative and positive memories. *European Journal of Psychotraumatology*, *1*, 5623.

Harber, V. J., & Sutton, J. R. (1984). Endorphins and exercise. *Sports Medicine*, *1*(2), 154–171.

Pearce, W. B. (1994). *Interpersonal communication: Making social worlds*. HarperCollins.

Pearce, W. B. (2004). The coordinated management of meaning (CMM). In B. William (Ed.), *Theorising about intercultural communication* (Chapter 2). Gudykunst

Rodriguez-Ayllon, M., Cadenas-Sánchez, C., Estévez-López, F., Muñoz, N. E., Mora-Gonzalez, J., Migueles, J. H., & Esteban-Cornejo, I. (2019). Role of physical activity and sedentary behaviour in the mental health of preschoolers, children and adolescents: A systematic review and meta-analysis. *Sports Medicine*, *49*(9), 1383–1410.

Sells, S. (2019). *Safety first before trauma treatment*. Family Trauma Institute.

Shapiro, F. (1989). Eye movement desensitisation: A new treatment for post-traumatic stress disorder. *Journal of Behaviour Therapy and Experimental Psychiatry*, *20*(3), 211–217.

Shotter, J. (2015). On being dialogical: An ethics on 'attunement'. *Context*, *137*.

Van den Hout, M. A., Engelhard, I. M., Rijkeboer, M. M., Koekebakker, J., Hornsveld, H., Leer, A., et al. (2011). EMDR: Eye movements superior to beeps in taxing working memory and reducing vividness of recollections. *Behaviour Research and Therapy*, *49*, 92–98.

Van der Kolk, B. A. (1994). The body keeps the score: Memory and the evolving psychobiology of posttraumatic stress. *Harvard Review Psychiatry*, *1*(5), 253–265.

Voss, M. W., Vivar, C., Kramer, A. F., & van Praag, H. (2013). Bridging animal and human models of exercise-induced brain plasticity. *Trends Cognitive Sciences*, *17*, 525–544.

Wolpe, J. (1990). *The practice of behaviour therapy* (4th ed.). Pergamon Press.

Chapter 9

Amnesty International UK. (2021). *'Safe and legal routes' briefing*. See 'Safe and Legal Routes' Briefing. Amnesty International UK.

Article 22 of the United Nations Convention on the Rights of the Child. (1999). *See UNCRC child friendly version 1*. savethechildren.org.uk.

Bakhtin, M. M. (1993). *Towards a philosophy of the act* (V. Liapunov, Ed.). Austin University of Texas Press.

Bateson, G. (1967). Cybernetic explanation. *American Behavioral Scientist*, *10*(8), 29–29.

Bateson, G. (1972). *In steps to an ecology of mind*. Chandler Publishing Company.

Bateson, G., Jackson, D. D., Haley, J., & Weakland, J. (1956). Toward a theory of schizophrenia. *Behavioral Science*, *1*(4), 251–264.

Bhugra, D. (2020). *Oxford textbook of Migrant Psychiatry*. Oxford University Press.

Comas-Díaz, L., & Torres Rivera, E. (Eds.). (2020). *Liberation psychology: Theory, method, practice, and social justice*. American Psychological Association.

Doughty Street Chambers. (2023). *LinkedIn statement from their Children's Rights Group and its Public Law*. Immigration and Community Care Teams.

Grimm, R. H. (1979). Circularity and self-reference in Nietzsche. *Metaphilosophy*, *10*, 289–305.

Jensen, A., & Penman, R. (2018). CMM, a brief overview. *Cosmopolis*, *2045*.

Johnston, T., & Robinsons, P. (2017). *Grief work, continuing bonds and co-creating new stories*. CMMI Fellows.

Laenui, P. (2000). Process of decolonization. In M. Battiste (Ed.), *Reclaiming indigenous voice and vision* (pp. 156–160). UBC Press.

Lang, P., Little, M., & Cronen, V. (1990). The systemic professional domains of action and the question of neutrality. *Human Systems: The Journal of Systemic Consultation & Management*, *1*, 39–55.

Martin-Baro, I. (1994). *Writings for liberation psychology* (A. Aron & S. Corne, Eds.). Harvard University Press.

Maturana, H. (1985). *Oxford conversations*. Conference jointly organised by Kensington Consultation Centre, London, The Family Institute, Cardiff, and The Charles Burns Clinic, Birmingham.

Mbembe, A. (2021). *Out of the dark night: Essays on decolonization*. Columbia University Press.

Morgan, D. L. (2018). Living within blurry boundaries: The value of distinguishing between qualitative and quantitative research. *Journal of Mixed Methods Research*, *12*(3), 268–279.

Pearce, W. B. (1994). *Interpersonal communication: Making social worlds*. HarperCollins.

Pearce, W. B. (2006). *Doing research from the perspective of the coordinated management of meaning.* Tao Institute.

Pearce, W. B., & Pearce, K. A. (1990). Transcendent storytelling: Abilities for systemic practitioners and their clients. *Human Systems, 9*(3–4), 167–185.

Ponte, P., & Smit, B. H. J. (Eds.). (2007). *The quality of practitioner research: Reflections on the position of the researcher and the researched* (pp. 29–42). Sense Publishers. All rights reserved.

UK Politics. (2015). *British broadcasting corporation.* David Cameron: 'Swarm' of Migrants Crossing Mediterranean – BBC News.

The United Nations Human Rights Commission. (2023). *About human rights and trafficking in person.* See OHCHR and trafficking in persons. OHCHR.

White, M., & Epston, D. (1990). *Narrative means to therapeutic ends.* Norton Books.

World Health Organisation. (2019). *Delivering quality health services: A global imperative for universal health coverage.* World Health Organization, Organisation for Economic Co-operation and Development, and The World Bank.

Index

Note: Page numbers in *italic* indicate a figure and page numbers in **bold** indicate a table on the corresponding page.

For Product Safety Concerns and Information please contact our EU
representative GPSR@taylorandfrancis.com
Taylor & Francis Verlag GmbH, Kaufingerstraße 24, 80331 München, Germany